APPLETON'S POPULAR LIBRARY.

OF THE BEST AUTHORS.

LIVES OF WELLINGTON AND PEEL.

LIVES

OF

WELLINGTON AND PEEL.

FROM THE LONDON TIMES.

NEW-YORK:
D. APPLETON & COMPANY, 200 BROADWAY.
1852.

PUBLISHERS' ADVERTISEMENT.

THE following Biographies appeared in the *London Times* immediately upon the announcement of the deaths of their illustrious subjects. They are here reprinted in full, accompanied with the leading articles from the same journal expressive of the sentiments of the occasion. The newspaper of the day has probably never afforded a more complete or distinguished contribution to historical literature. The condensation of facts is admirable, presenting what every reader of intelligence just now demands, an able and comprehensive review of the many incidents of the career of England's great soldier and statesman of the present century Without seeking points of affinity in the course of the two, or looking beyond the reader's convenience in the preparation of this volume, there may yet be a propriety in the arrangement of these biographies from the personal relations of Peel and Wellington.

"It is an interesting fact," observes a London journal, "that when the first passages in the Peninsular campaigns were severely criticised in Parliament, a young man, the son of a manufacturer, defended them again and again with admirable talent and great readiness in debate. This was the late Sir Robert Peel, whose epitaph the Duke of Wellington lived to speak nobly and touchingly in the House of Lords.

NEW YORK, *Oct.*, 1852.

CONTENTS.

LIVES

OF

WELLINGTON AND PEEL.

ARTHUR WELLESLEY,

DUKE OF WELLINGTON.

It is a circumstance of rather unusual occurrence that the day and place of a famous birth should be unknown even to contemporary inquirers; yet such is the case on the present occasion. It is certain that the Duke of Wellington was born in Ireland, and of an Irish family, and that the year in which he saw the light was that which ushered also Napoleon Bonaparte into the world. For most purposes but those of astrology these verifications of fact would be sufficient; but it is not unlikely that the event which has now thrown Britain into mourning, may reanimate a controversy not without its attractions to inquisitive minds. The 1st of May, 1769, is specified, with few variations, as the birthday of Arthur Wellesley by those of his biographers who venture on such circumstantiality, and Dangan Castle, county of Meath, has been selected with similar unanimity as the place of the event. The former of these statements has received a kind of confirmation by the adoption of the Duke's name and sponsorship for a

Royal infant born on the day in question; yet, in the registry of St. Peter's Church, Dublin, it is duly recorded that "Arthur, son of the Right Hon. Earl and Countess of Mornington," was there christened by "Isaac Maun, archdeacon, on the 30th of April, 1769." This entry, while it conclusively negatives one of the two foregoing presumptions, materially invalidates the other also; for, though not impossible, it is certainly not likely that the infant, if born at Dangan, would have been baptized in Dublin. Our own information leads us to believe that the illustrious subject of this biography first saw the light in the town residence of his parents, Mornington-house, a mansion of some pretensions in the centre of the eastern side of Upper Merrion-street, Dublin, and which, as it abutted 80 years ago as a corner house upon a large area, since enclosed with buildings, was occasionally described as situate in Merrion-square. We are not inclined, however, to pursue a question of which the most notable point is the indifference with which it was treated by the person most immediately concerned. The Duke kept his birthday on the 18th of June.

Two families, both English by original extraction, and but Irish by settlement and adoption, were centred in the lineage from which our great Captain sprung. We shall be giving sufficient prominence to points possessing little beyond incidental interest if we state that in the year 1728 Richard Colley, of Castle Carbery, in the county of Kildare, succeeded to the name and estates of Garret Wesley, of Dangan Castle, in the county of Meath. The Colleys had migrated in the 16th century from Rutlandshire; the Wesleys at an earlier date from

Sussex. The two families had been already connected by a recent alliance, so that Richard Colley was the first cousin of Garret Wesley, whose estates in default of lineal issue he was called to inherit. The former of these two names was indiscriminately specified as Cooley, Colley, or Cowley; the third of which forms obtained the preference at a recent revival of the family designation; the latter was usually written Westley or Wesley till 1797, when the first Marquis adopted the orthography of Wellesley, now familiar to the world. It was, however, as "Arthur Wesley" that the subject of these memoirs was first known as a soldier, and the young officer will be found so designated in contemporary descriptions of his earlier services. The double notoriety attaching itself to the name of Wesley will be suggestive, we doubt not, of some edifying thoughts, and to the ready pen which chronicled both reputations in the respective history of Methodism and the Peninsular War, we owe an anecdote curious enough to be transcribed into our more concise biography. When Charles, the brother of John Wesley, was at Westminster School, his father received a communication from an Irish gentleman, offering to adopt the boy as heir; but the overture, strange as it may seem, was declined. It was for this Charles Wesley that Richard Colley was substituted by the owner of Dangan, and thus, but for a capricious and improbable transfer of fortune, "we might," says Southey in his speculative reflections, "have had no Methodists; the British empire in India might still have been menaced from Seringapatam, and the undisputed tyrant of Europe might still have insulted and threatened us on our own shores." The Richard

Colley thus favoured was created Baron Mornington, of the Irish peerage, in 1746, a title which was exchanged for an earldom, 14 years later, in favour of his son. This second Lord Mornington, of musical celebrity, left by his wife, Anne, daughter of Arthur Hill, Viscount Dungannon, nine children surviving, of whom one became Marquis Wellesley, one Baron Cowley, and one, christened we presume after his maternal grandfather, Duke of Wellington.

Arthur Wellesley, by the death of his father in 1781, became dependent at an early age upon the care and prudence of his mother, a lady, as it fortunately happened, of talents not unequal to the task. Under this direction of his studies he was sent to Eton, from which college he was transferred, first, to private tuition at Brighton, and subsequently to the military seminary of Angers, in France. For the deficiency of any early promise in the future hero we are not confined to negative evidence alone. His relative inferiority was the subject of some concern to his vigilant mother, and had its influence, as we are led to conclude, in the selection of the military profession for one who displayed so little of the family aptitude for elegant scholarship. At Angers, though the young student left no signal reputation behind him, it is clear that his time must have been productively employed. Pignerol, the director of the seminary, was an engineer of high repute, and the opportunities of acquiring, not only professional knowledge, but a serviceable mastery of the French tongue, were not likely to have been lost on such a mind as that of his pupil. Altogether, six years were consumed in this course of education, which, though partial enough in itself, was so far in advance of the age that we may conceive the young cadet to have carried with him to his corps a more than average store of professional acquirements. On the 7th of March, 1787, the Hon. Arthur Wellesley, being then in his 18th year, received his first commission as an ensign in the 73d Regiment of Foot. The only point of interest in his position at this minute is the degree of advantage over his contemporaries which might be derived from the family connexions above described; and a review of the facts will lead, we think, to the conclusion that, though the young officer commanded sufficient interest to bring his deserts into immediate and favourable notice, he was not so circumstanced as to rely exclusively on such considerations for advancement. A French historian, indeed, has indulged in a sneer at the readiness with which the haughty aristocracy of Britain submitted themselves, in after times, to the ascendancy of an Irish *parvenu*, but this assumption is as little warrantable as that by which the distinctions of the young cadet are attributed to the nobility of his extraction. The pretensions of Arthur Wellesley were insufficient, even at a somewhat later period, to secure him from failure in that test of social position—the choice of a wife; nor could his opportunities have produced more than commonplace success to a man of ordinary capacity. On the other hand, they relieved him from those risks of neglect and injustice which must occasionally be fatal even to eminent worth, and they carried him rapidly over those early stages in which, under other circumstances, the fortunes of a life might have been perhaps consumed. He possessed interest enough to make merit available, but not enough to dispense with it.

His promotion was accordingly rapid, but not more so in its first steps than in examples visible at the present day, and much less so than in the case of some of his contemporaries. He remained a subaltern four years and three months, at the expiration of which period of service he received his captaincy. The honour of having trained the Duke of Wellington would be highly regarded in the traditions of any particular corps, but so numerous and rapid were his exchanges at this period that the distinction can hardly be claimed by any of the regiments on the rolls of which he was temporarily borne. He entered the army, as we have said, in the 73d, but in the same year he moved, as lieutenant, to the 76th, and within the next eighteen months was transferred, still in a subaltern's capacity, to the 41st foot and the 12th Light Dragoons, successively. On the 30th of June, 1791, he was promoted to a captaincy in the 58th, from which corps he exchanged into the 18th Light Dragoons in the October of the following year. At length, on the 30th of April, 1793, he obtained his majority in the 33d, a regiment which may boast of considerable indentification with his renown, for he proceeded in it to his lieutenant-colonelcy and colonelcy, and commanded it personally throughout the early stages of his active career. These rapid exchanges bespeak the operation of somewhat unusual interest in pushing the young officer forward; for in those days a soldier ordinarily continued in the corps to which he was first gazetted, and to which his hopes, prospects, and connections were mainly confined. So close, indeed, and permanent were the ties thus formed, that when Colonel Wellesley's own comrade and commander, General Harris, was asked to name the title by which he would desire to enter the peerage, he could only refer to the 5th Fusiliers as having been for nearly six and twenty years his constant home. The brother of Lord Mornington was raised above these necessities of routine; but what is chiefly noticeable in the incidents described is that the period of his probationary service was divided between cavalry and infantry alike—a circumstance of some advantage to so observant a mind.

Before the active career of the young officer commenced he was attached as aide-de-camp to the staff of the Earl of Westmoreland, then Lord-Lieutenant of Ireland, and in 1790, having just come of age, he was returned to the Irish Parliament for the family borough of Trim. The most eager researches into this period of his career, have not elicited any thing to prove that he was distinguished from those around him. In one particular, indeed, he shared the failings common to his class and times, after a fashion singularly contrasted with the subsequent developments of his character. Captain Wellesley got seriously into debt. So pressing, in fact, were his obligations, that he accepted temporary relief from a bootmaker in whose house he lodged; and before quitting England on foreign service confided the arrangement of his affairs to another Dublin tradesman, whom he empowered for this purpose to receive the disposable portion of his income.

At length, in the month of May, 1794, Arthur Wellesley, being then in his twenty-sixth year and in command of the 33d Regiment—a position which he owed to his brother's liberality—embarked at Cork for service on the continent of Europe, so that his first active duties involved great independent responsibility. The aspect of affairs at that period was unpromising in the extreme. War had been declared about twelve months previously between England and France, and 10,000 British troops, under the command of the Duke of York, had been despatched to aid the operations of the Allied Powers in the Low Countries. It would be difficult to impress an Englishman of the present generation with a true conception of the character and reputation of the British army at that period. Forty years had elapsed since the appearance of any considerable English force on the European continent, and the recollections of the campaigns in question were not calculated to suggest any high opinions of British prowess. In fact, the Duke of Cumberland had been systematically beaten by Marshal Saxe, and the traditions of Marlborough's wars had been obliterated by contests in which the superiority of the French soldiery seemed to be declared. The ascendancy, too, so signally acquired at this time by our navy tended to confirm the impressions referred to, and it was argued that the ocean had been clearly marked out as the exclusive scene of our preponderance. Throughout a great part of the century these opinions had been rather justified than belied by our own proceedings. We fought many of our colonial battles with mercenaries, and we hired German battalions even to defend our coasts and protect the established succession of the Throne. A new school of war, to which the attention of the reader will be presently directed, was, indeed, forming in the East; but its influence was hardly yet known, and the Duke of York's corps was disembarked at Ostend with, perhaps, less prestige than any division of the allied army. Though the exertions of the Royal commander had already been directed, and with some success, to military reforms, yet the conditions of the service were still miserably bad. The commissariat was wretched, the medical department shamefully ineffective, and rapacity, peculation, and mismanagement prevailed to a most serious extent. Such was the army which Colonel Wellesley proceeded to join. It was no wonder that English as well as Imperialists were worsted by Republican levies, not only numerically superior, but whose system confounded all received tactics as utterly as the campaigns of Charles VIII. in Italy demolished the conceptions of mediæval warfare. The Duke of York was repulsed in a series of engagements which we need not describe, and it was in aid of his discomfited force that Colonel Wellesley carried out the 33d Regiment to the scene of his first, as well as of his last service—the plains of Belgium.

The first military operation performed by the conqueror of Waterloo was the evacuation of a town in the face of the enemy. The 33d had been landed at Ostend; but when Lord Moira, who had the chief command of the reinforcements sent out, arrived at that port with the main body, he saw reason for promptly withdrawing the garrison and abandoning the place. Orders were issued accordingly, and though the Republicans, under Pichegru, were at the gates of the town before the English had quitted it, the 33d was safely embarked. Lord Moira by a flank march effected a timely junction with the Duke of York at Malines.

Colonel Wellesley took his corps round by the Scheldt, and landed at Antwerp, whence he moved without delay to the head-quarters of the Duke. This was in July, 1794. The operations which followed, and which terminated in the following spring with the re-embarcation of the British troops at Bremerlehe, a town at the mouth of the Weser, constituted Arthur Wellesley's first campaign. They do not, for the purposes of our memoir, require any circumstantial description. The total force of the Allied Powers was strong, but it was extended over a long line of country, composed of heterogeneous troops, and commanded by generals, not only independent, but suspicious of each other's decisions. In the face of an enemy, first animated by desperation and then intoxicated by success, there existed no unity of plan or concert of movements. After the defeat sustained by the Austrians at Fleurus the campaign was resolved into retreat on the part of the Allies and pursuit of fortune on the part of the French. The Austrians were on the middle Rhine, the British on the Meuse. The route taken by the Duke of York in his successive retirements from one position to another lay through Breda, Bois le Duc, and Nimeguen, at which latter place he maintained himself against the enemy with some credit. Early in December, however, he resigned his command to General Walmoden, and returned to England, leaving the unfortunate division to struggle with even greater difficulties than they had yet experienced. Disengaged by repeated triumphs from their Austrian antagonists, the Republican forces closed in tremendous strength round the English and their comrades. The winter set in with such excessive severity that the rivers were passable for the heaviest class of cannon, provisions were scanty, and little aid was forthcoming from the inhabitants against either the inclemency of the season or the casualties of war. It was found necessary to retire into Westphalia, and in this retreat, which was commenced on the 15th of January, 1795, the troops are said to have endured for some days privations and sufferings little short of those encountered by the French in the Moscow campaign. So deep was the snow that all traces of roads were lost, wagons laden with sick and wounded were unavoidably abandoned, and to straggle from the column was to perish. The enemy were in hot pursuit, and the population undisguisedly hostile to their nominal allies. At length the Yssel was crossed, and the troops reposed for awhile in cantonments along the Ems; but as the French still prepared to push forward, the allied force continued its retreat, and as they entered Westphalia the tardy appearance of a strong Prussian corps secured them from further molestation till the embarcation took place.

Such was the Duke of Wellington's first campaign. Whatever might have been the actual precocity of his talent, there was obviously no room in such operations for the exercise on his part of anything beyond intrepidity and steadiness, and these qualities, as we learn, were made visibly manifest. His post was that which in a retreat is the post of honour—the rearguard. The command of a brigade devolved on him by seniority, and the able dispositions of Colonel Wellesley in checking the enemy or executing an assault are circumstances of special remark in contemporary accounts of the transactions. In particular, the affairs of Druyten, Meteren, and Geldermansel, are mentioned with some detail, as reflecting considerable credit on the 33d and its commander. Beyond this point Colonel Wellesley's reputation was not extended, but we may readily imagine how material a portion of his professional character might have been formed in this Dutch campaign. Irrespectively of the general uses of adversity, the miscarriages of this ill-starred expedition must have been fraught with invaluable lessons to the future hero. He observed the absolute need of undivided authority in an enemy's presence, and the hopelessness of all such imperfect combinations as State jealousies suggested. We are justified in inferring from his subsequent demonstrations of character that no error escaped either his notice or his memory. He saw a powerful force frittered away by divisions, and utterly routed by an enemy which but a few months before had been scared at the very news of its approach. He saw the indispensability of preserving discipline in a friendly country, and of conciliating the dispositions of a local population, always powerful for good or evil. Though a master hand was wanting at head-quarters, yet Abercromby was present, and the young Picton was making his first essay by the side of his future comrade. Austrian, Prussian, Hanoverian, French, Dutch, and British were in the field together, and the care exemplified in appointing and provisioning the respective battalions might be serviceably contrasted. Every check, every repulse, every privation, and every loss brought, we may be sure, its enduring moral to Arthur Wellesley; and although Englishmen may not reflect without emotion on the destinies which were thus perilled in the swamps of Holland, the future General had perhaps little reason to repine at the rugged tuition of his first campaign.

On the return of the expedition to England the 33d was landed at Harwich, and for a short time encamped at Warley, where it soon recovered its effective strength. In the autumn of the same year Colonel Wellesley conducted his corps to Southampton, where it was embarked on board the outward-bound fleet, under the flag of Admiral Christian. The destination of the force was the West Indies, but through a series of accidents so remarkable as to acquire, in conjunction with subsequent events, a providential character, the orders were ultimately changed, and the services of the young Colonel were employed on a scene far better calculated to develope his military genius. For some time the winds were so adverse that the vessels were unable to quit the port at all, and when they had at length succeeded in putting to sea they encountered such tempestuous weather as to be finally compelled, after experiencing serious casualties, to return to Portsmouth. Meantime new exigencies had arisen, and in the spring of 1796 the weather-beaten 33d received directions to embark for Bengal. At this critical period, however, the health of Colonel Wellesley suddenly failed him. Considering that strength of constitution and temperament with which we have since become familiar, it is remarkable to observe how repeatedly the Iron Duke, in earlier days, was attacked, and apparently almost mastered, by debility and sickness. On the present occasion he was actually unable to embark with his regiment, but a favourable change afterwards supervened, and he succeeded in joining the corps at the Cape of Good Hope. The remainder of the voyage was soon completed, and in February, 1797, Arthur Wellesley landed at Calcutta to commence in earnest that career of service which will reflect such eternal lustre on his name.

Before recounting those memorable campaigns by which our empire in the East was finally established, it will be desirable to premise some intelligible description of the scenes and persons to which Colonel Wellesley was now introduced. Half the unpopularity attributed to Indian history resides in the strangeness of Oriental names, and we are persuaded that any reader of ordinary attention who would familiarise himself with the geographical expressions and family titles current in these parts, would afterwards comprehend the affairs of India with as much readiness as those of any European country.

In 1797 there still existed, and in something more than name, a Great Mogul, that is to say, a representative of that Mogul or Tartar dynasty which since the commencement of the 16th century had established itself in the Imperial Sovereignty of India. He was not, however, directly possessed of any substantial power, though there was eager competition for the exercise of his traditional authority. He resided at Delhi, and in histories of this period is often termed "the King," a title which, though afterwards conferred by us on the Nabob of Oude, was long considered in India as the exclusive property of the supreme territorial lord. The power lost by this monarch in the decline of his dominion had been seized by two classes of people—his own lieutenants, who had converted their governments into independent heritages; and his Hindoo subjects, who had embraced the opportunity of renouncing an allegiance which they had never willingly or perhaps absolutely acknowledged. Of the former class were the Nabobs of Oude and Bengal in Hindostan, *i. e.*, in that part of India, commonly so called, which is north of the Nerbudda river, and the still more powerful lieutenant who administered singly the whole of the "Deccan" or "South," under which designation was nominally comprised almost all the southern portion of the peninsular exclusive of "the Carnatic," a name attached to its south-eastern districts between the river Kistnah and Cape Comorin. The first of these Princes was usually termed "the Nabob-Vizier," or "Vizier," in consequence of that office having been monopolised by his family during the decline of the Mogul empire. The second, the "Nabob" or "Subahdar" of Bengal, had been conquered by us at Plassey, and we had virtually assumed his inheritance ourselves. The third, he of the Deccan, was termed "the Nizam," or "Lieutenant," —a title which had been given purely for personal distinction to the first Viceroy of this province on his accepting office, but which had been perpetuated in favour of his successors, as we see to this day. The Carnatic was not held immediately of the Mogul Sovereign, but of his lieutenant in the Deccan, who thus claimed the allegiance of a feudatory not greatly inferior to himself. The Prince in question was called the Nabob of the Carnatic, or, more familiarly, from his place of residence, the Nabob of Arcot. These were the Mahometan Powers with which we had then to deal.

The Hindoo pretenders to dominion were represented by the Mahrattas, a powerful and warlike tribe of the Malabar coast, which had successfully resisted the great Aurungzebe, and which had turned to such profit the imbecility of his successors as to have almost revived in their own favor the Imperial claims of the Moguls themselves. They had extended their power by dispatching their great captains in various directions on the common errand of conquest; such conquests to be retained by the individual victors on condition of allegiance and tribute payable to the supreme family. This family held court originally at Sattara, under a title which has been made familiar to the present generation by the importunities of its *soi-disant* representative; but the Rajahs of Sattara had been superseded in all effective or cognizable authority by the "Peishwa" or "chief" of their own privy council—an office which had been made hereditary in a particular family, and to which the princely power had been wholly transferred. The Peishwa resided at Poonah, but his lieutenants had already assumed an independence little less substantial than that of the Mogul viceroys just described. One named Scindiah, then the most formidable of the cousinhood, had established himself in Malwa, and was pretending to extraordinary dominion in western Hindostan; another, named Holkar, had set up his standard a little to the south of Scindiah, in the town of Indore; the Bhonsla family were settled with great possessions at Nagpore, in the north-east of the Deccan; and the "Guicowar," or "herdsman," was installed in the government of Guzerat, contiguous to the Peishwa's territory. Of this great and formidable Mahratta confederacy only two members now survive as substantive powers of India—the Guicowar, still called by his ancestral appellative; and the Nagpore prince, at present styled the Rajah of Berar; the Peishwa's prerogatives having been extinguished and absorbed by Lord Hastings in 1819, and Scindiah and Holkar having succumbed in the stubborn contests which we shall have presently to recount. It will further be requisite to mention that an inconsiderable Hindoo principality in the south had been usurped by a Mahometan adventurer, who was consolidating an inheritance with true Oriental success, and that the Abdalla empire, founded about 40 years previously in Affghanistan, was still vigorously administered by Zemaum Shah, the identical prince visited by our own generals but the other day. Our remarks refer to a period of Indian history so comparatively early, that any actor in these half-forgotten scenes appears like a phantom of the past; but it will stimulate our interest in the subject before us, if we endeavour to realize to our own imaginations that the grey-headed old soldier who but yesterday was riding down Whitehall was the identical hero who fifty years since drove Dowlut Rao to capitulate, and packed off Dhoondiah on the carriage of a galloper gun. It is strange that the commander of an army should be one of its last survivors.

The position of the Indian Government relatively to the Home Administration was not, when Colonel Wellesley arrived in those parts, materially different from that which exists at present. The great step of identifying these prodigious acquisitions with the dominions of the British Crown had virtually been taken already; and Lord Cornwallis, in the last war, had wielded, to

Tippoo's cost, the resources of an Empire instead of the arms of a Company. A few years earlier India had scarcely been reputed among the fields open to the soldiers of the British army, and regiments were reluctantly despatched to quarters not looked upon at first with any favourable eye. But the scene had been changed by late achievements; and though a command in India was not what it has since become, it was an object of reasonable ambition. Napoleon pretended, even after the victories of Seringapatam and Assaye, to slight the services of a "sepoy general," but Wellesley established for the school, in the eyes of all Europe, a reputation which it has never since lost.

Small as were the anticipations of such active service which the young Colonel could have entertained at his first landing in India, a few months saw him in the field with his corps against a resolute and formidable enemy. By a notable instance of fortune, the elder brother of Arthur Wellesley was nominated to the Governor-Generalship of India within a few months after the subject of these memoirs had arrived at Calcutta, and the talents of a most accomplished statesman were thus at hand to develope and reward the genius of the rising soldier. Lord Mornington, like many of his successors, went out in the confident expectation of maintaining peace, but found himself engaged in hostilities against his most ardent desire. At that time the three Presidencies of India shared pretty evenly between them the perils and prospects of active service in the field. Bengal, since the definite submission of Oude, had been comparatively quiet; but it was the Imperial presidency, and its troops were held readily disposable for the exigencies of the others. Bombay vibrated with every convulsion of the Mahratta States, by which it was surrounded; and Madras, in earlier times the leading government, had recovered much of its importance from the virtual absorption of the Carnatic, the formidable resources and uncertain disposition of the Nizam, and, above all, the menacing attitude of Tippoo Sultaun, the adventurer of Mysore. It was against this barbaric chieftain that the spurs of Arthur Wellesley were won.

When the two brothers met at Calcutta, in 1798, the principal risk of war was created by the unruly resentments of Tippoo. Oude had been subdued; Bengal was our own; the Carnatic had been absorbed, and the Nizam of the Deccan, like the other Princes still independent, was trimming between the British alliance and that of States whom he dreaded still more than ourselves. There still remained, however, a considerable element of *French* influence in the peninsula. We had, it is true, definitely expelled these dangerous rivals by the capture of Pondicherry in 1761, and they no longer worked openly on their own account; but the Nizam maintained an imposing force disciplined by more than 100 French officers, under M. Raymond, and Scindiah employed with similar views the services of General Perron. It can be little matter of surprise, therefore, that the dread of French influence should still predominate at Madras, and it was the assumed identification of Tippoo with these inveterate antagonists of Britain which rendered the wars with him, and with him *only* of all Indian Princes, so generally popular at home.

Tippoo had recently made peace with the Company,

but the treaty as regarded his stipulations was so essentially of a penal character that his patient acquiescence in its operation was not to be expected, though Lord Mornington, as we have seen, did both desire and anticipate a perpetuation of the truce. Within a very few weeks, however, of his arrival at the seat of his government, he learnt that the Mysore Sultaun had been actively intriguing with the French for the purpose of expelling us from the Peninsula. It is more likely, perhaps, that this idea should have been suggested to Tippoo by some one of the many Frenchmen still lurking in India than that the Oriental despot should of himself have descried the resources presented to him by the unscrupulous ambition of the Republican Directory. However this may be, he undoubtedly despatched ambassadors with this object to the Mauritius, the nearest French settlement, and these envoys actually disembarked at Mangalore on their return voyage, with a body of European recruits, at the very moment that the new Governor-General on his way to Calcutta touched at Madras. It does not fall within our purpose to discuss the respective cases of the belligerents. It is enough to remark that Tippoo's suspicions of ourselves were most cordially reciprocated, and that this new dynasty of Mysore had been always regarded, both in India and at home, with excessive jealousy and alarm. A war with Tippoo was counted as a life and death struggle, and although the last campaign of Cornwallis had pretty clearly prognosticated the ultimate issue, yet the whole resources of the Indian Government were now summoned as to a deadly strife. Those resolutions nearly affected the rising fortunes of Arthur Wellesley. On landing, as we have seen, at Calcutta in February, 1797, he had been despatched upon an expedition directed against Manilla, but transports sailed slowly in those days, and by the time that the several vessels had arrived at their first rendezvous the alarm had been given at Madras, and they were overtaken by a peremptory recall. Each Presidency mustered its whole strength for the conflict, and as a reinforcement of that most immediately menaced, the 33d was transferred from Bengal and placed upon the Madras establishment. On this new scene of duty Colonel Wellesley arrived in September, 1798.

It had happened, and, as we may reasonably conclude, by something more than accident, that the young Colonel was already well acquainted with the future theatre of war. On returning from the Straits he had paid a visit to Lord Hobart, then Governor of Madras. His stay extended over a few weeks only; but this short period had enabled him to cast his eagle glance over the military establishments of that Presidency, and over the various capabilities of the Carnatic. He brought, therefore, to the duties which he now assumed, information of a most serviceable character. The Commander-in-Chief at Madras was General, afterwards Lord Harris, under whose auspices Colonel Wellesley was stationed at Wallajahbad, with the responsible commission of organizing, equipping, and practising the forces of the Presidency destined for the expedition. Ths state of feeling in India at that period partook of no such confidence as was afterwards displayed. The troops at the Governor's command were neither numerous nor well provided; the resources of the Treasury were scanty, and the alliances of the Company had been seriously damaged by the temporizing and ungenerous policy of the late Governor-General, Sir John Shore. Moreover, although the last campaign had been undoubtedly successful in its results, recollections of a disagreeable character were created by its vast consumption of blood and treasure, and by the perils of miscarriage which had been experienced in its course. It is natural enough from our present point of view to consider these apprehensions as having been unduly magnified, but it should be remembered at the very moment when Colonel Wellesley was ordered to Madras, Bonaparte had actually disembarked a French army on the shores of Egypt, and had put himself in communication with Tippoo—facts quite menacing enough to warrant unusual misgivings. The strength, too, of the Mysore army gave at least 70,000 troops, admirably equipped, and in no contemptible state of discipline, while the Madras muster rolls showed a total of no more than 14,000 of all arms, including less than 4,000 Europeans. In fact, Lord Mornington had been compelled to exchange the scheme of attack originally contemplated for a more cautious and regular exertion of his strength. With these reluctant conclusions he ordered General Harris to stand on the defensive along the Mysore frontier, and to augment the efficiency of his army by all available means, while he turned his own attention to the native Courts, whose alliance or neutrality it was desirable to secure.

That nothing on his part might be wanting to the success of the enterprise, he had transferred himself and his staff from Calcutta to Madras, and the effects of his policy and his presence were quickly discernible in the impulse communicated to every department of the service, and the restoration of energy and confidence throughout the Presidency. These efforts were admirably seconded by the practical exertions of his brother at Wallajahbad. So effectually had Colonel Wellesley employed the three months of his local command, that the division under his charge from being weak and ill provided had become conspicuous for its organization and equipment, and when the whole army presently took the field in unparalleled efficiency, the especial services of Colonel Wellesley in bringing about this result were acknowledged in a general order of the Commander-in-Chief. The whole force now put in motion against the famous Tiger of Mysore comprised three divisions—that of the Carnatic, 30,000 strong, that of Bombay, two-thirds less numerous, and the contingent of our ally, the Nizam. The latter consisted of the British detachment in the Nizam's service, of a few battalions of his own infantry, including some of M. Raymond's force lately disbanded, and of a large body of cavalry. To complete the efficiency of this powerful division it was resolved to add a King's regiment to its rolls, and at the express wish of the Nizam's Minister, coupled with the prompt approval of General Harris, Colonel Wellesley's corps was selected for this duty, and on him the general command of the whole contingent was suffered to devolve. By these arrangements, which were to the unqualified satisfaction of all parties concerned, Colonel Wellesley assumed a prominent place in the conduct of the war, and enjoyed opportunities of displaying both his special intelligence and his intuitive military powers. Few opportunities indeed could be better calculated for the full development of his genius. He held a command sufficiently independent to elicit all his talents; he formed one of the political commission attached to the Commander-in-Chief; and he acted under the eyes of a Governor whose acuteness in discerning merit and promptitude in rewarding it were quickened on this occasion by the natural impulses of affection. Nor were there wanting in the same ranks either models of excellence or stout competitors for fame. Besides Harris himself, there were Baird and Cotton, Dallas and Brown, Floyd and Malcolm—soldiers all of them of high distinction and extraordinary renown, who either sought or staked a professional reputation in this memorable war against Tippoo Sultaun.

By the end of February, 1799, the invading forces had penetrated into the dominions of Mysore, though so difficult was the country and so insufficient, notwithstanding the previous preparations, were the means of transport, that half-a-dozen miles constituted an ordinary day's march, and three weeks were consumed in conveying intelligence from the western division of the army to the eastern. The first movements of Tippoo from his central position had been judiciously directed against the weaker corps which was advancing from Cananore, but in his attempt on this little force he was signally repulsed; on which, wheeling to the right about, and retracing his steps, he brought himself face to face with the main army under General Harris near Malavelly, a place within 30 miles of his capital city, Seringapatam. His desires to engage were promptly met by the British Commander, who received his attack with the right wing of the army, leaving the left, which was composed of the Nizam's contingent under Colonel Wellesley, to charge and turn the flank of the enemy opposed to it. Colonel Wellesley's dispositions for this assault were speedily made, and, having been approved by General Harris, were executed with complete success. The conduct of the 33d decided the action. Knowing that if he could break the European regiment the native battalions might be expected to despair, the Sultaun directed a column of his choicest troops against Colonel Wellesley's corps; which, reserving its fire till the enemy had closed, delivered a searching volley, charged, and threw the whole column into a disorder which the sabres of the Dragoons were not long in converting to a rout. After this essay it was clear that the campaign would turn upon the siege of the capital, and on the 4th of April the army, by the judicious strategy of Harris, arrived in effective condition before the ramparts of Seringapatam.

Between the camp of the besiegers and the walls of this famous fortress stretched a considerable extent of irregular and broken ground, affording excellent cover to the enemy for annoying the British lines with musketry and rocket practice. At one extremity was a "tope" or grove called the Sultaunpettah tope, composed mainly of betel trees, and intersected by numerous water-courses for the purposes of irrigation. The first operations of the besiegers were directed to the occupation of a position so peculiarly serviceable to the party maintaining it. Accordingly, on the night of the 4th General Baird was ordered to scour this tope--a commission which he discharged without encountering any opposition. Next morning Tippoo's troops were again seen to occupy it in great force, on which General Harris resolved to repeat the attack on the succeeding night, and to retain the position when carried. The duty was intrusted on this occasion to Colonel Wellesley of the 33d and a native battalion, who was to be supported by another detachment of similar strength under Colonel Shawe. This was the famous affair of which so much has been said, and which, with such various colourings, has been described as the first service of Arthur, Duke of Wellington. On receiving the order, Colonel Wellesley addressed to his commander the following note, remarkable as being the first of that series of despatches which now constitute so extraordinary a monument of his fame:—

"TO LIEUTENANT-GENERAL HARRIS, COMMANDER-IN-CHIEF.

"*Camp, 5th April*, 1799.

"MY DEAR SIR,—I do not know where you mean the post to be established, and I shall therefore be obliged to you if you will do me the favour to meet me this afternoon in front of the lines and show it to me. In the meantime I will order my battalion to be in readiness.

"Upon looking at the tope as I came in just now, it appeared to me that when you get possession of the bank of the nullah you have the tope as a matter of course, as the latter is in the rear of the former. However, you are the best judge, and I shall be ready.

"I am, my dear Sir, your most faithful servant,

"ARTHUR WELLESLEY."

This letter has been often appealed to as evidence of that brevity, perspicacity, and decision afterwards recognized as such notable characteristics of the great Duke's style. Without stopping to challenge the criticism, we would rather point to it as signally exemplifying the change which had taken place in the young Colonel's official position since we last saw him in the Dutch campaign. Instead of simply conducting a regiment, we now find him, though still only a colonel, in command of a powerful division of an army, influencing the character of its operations, corresponding on terms of freedom with the General-in-Chief, and preserving his despatches for the edification of posterity. Reserving, however, any further comment on these circumstances, we must now state that the attack in question was a failure. Bewildered in the darkness of the night, and entangled in the difficulties of the tope, the assaulting parties were thrown into confusion, and, although Shawe was enabled to report himself in possession of the post assigned to him, Colonel Wellesley was compelled, as the General records in his private diary, to come, "in a good deal of agitation, to say he had not carried the tope." When daylight broke the attack was renewed with instantaneous success, showing at once what had been the nature of the obstacles on the previous night; but the affair has been frequently quoted as Wellington's "only failure," and the particulars of the occurrence were turned to some account in the jealousies and scandals from which no camp is wholly free. The reader will at once perceive that the circumstances suggest no discussion whatever. A night attack, by the most natural of results, failed of its object, and was successfully executed the next morning as soon as the troops discovered the nature of their duties.

When these advanced posts had fallen into our hands, the last hour of Tippoo's reign might be thought to have struck, and the final results of the expedition to be beyond peril. But there is an aspect of facility about Indian campaigning which is extremely delusive to those unexperienced in its risks. All goes apparently without a check, and all is thought easy and insignificant; but the truth is, that a single check, however slight, will often turn the whole tide of success. It is the characteristic of this warfare that reverses which in other countries would be endured without serious damage are here liable to be fatal. To our check before the little fort of Kalunga, in 1814, we owed probably the duration and losses of the Nepaul war, and it has been credibly averred that if the ingenious operations of our officers had failed before the gates of Ghuznee, the disasters of the Cabul retreat would have been anticipated in that first Affghan expedition, which now reads like a triumphal march. It is true that Tippoo's forces proved unequal to encounter in the field even the weakest of the invading armies, and that our position before Seringapatam had been taken up without any resistance proportioned to the renown or resources of our enemy. But the fort was extremely strong, the place unhealthy to the last degree, and any material protraction of the siege would have exhausted the provisions of the army, and given time for the season to do its work. The river Cauvery is periodically swelled during the monsoon, and, had this occurred earlier than usual, the siege must have been raised, and a disastrous retreat—for in India all retreats are disastrous—must have been the inevitable consequence. As it was, the

Commander-in-Chief was full of apprehensions, and Sir John Malcolm used in after days to relate an anecdote which shows better than any calculation how many chances still remained in Tippoo's favour. On the day appointed for the storm, he entered the General's tent, and saluted him by anticipation with the title which proved afterwards the reward of his services. "Malcolm," was the serious reply of the old chief, "this is no time for compliments. We have serious work on hand. Don't you see that the European sentry over my tent is so weak from want of food and exhaustion that a Sepoy could push him down? We must take this fort or perish in the attempt. I have ordered Baird to persevere in his attack to the last extremity; if he is beat off, Wellesley is to proceed with the troops from the trenches; if he also should not succeed, I shall put myself at the head of the remainder of the army, for success is necessary to our existence."

In fact, these arrangements had been actually made. Colonel Wellesley, whose unremitting attention to all the duties of the siege is shown in a multiplicity of despatches, and the value of whose suggestions is proved by their effect upon the operations, received orders to head the reserve in the advanced trenches and to await the success of the storm. The fighting in the batteries had already been desperate and the losses heavy, but 2,500 Europeans still survived to lead the assault, and a chosen column of Sepoys followed them. It was midday on the 4th of May. Colonel Wellesley had received reports of the state of the breach, had revised them in terms exactly like those afterwards used at Ciudad Rodrigo and Badajoz, had superintended the final preparations, and was expecting the result from his appointed post. "It was," says one near him, "a moment of agony, and we continued with aching eyes to watch the result, until, after a short and appalling interval, we saw the acclivity of the breach covered with a cloud of crimson." The assault succeeded, and Colonel Wellesley advanced from his position, not to renew a desperate attempt, but to restore some order in the captured city, and to certify the death of cur dreaded enemy by discovering his body yet warm and palpitating under a mountain of slain.

Duties little less arduous than those of the actual storm devolved presently upon the troops of the reserve and their commander. The captured city presented a scene of rapine, terror, and confusion, in which not even the conquerors were safe, and the despatches of Colonel Wellesley from within the walls to General Harris, who still remained without, assumed an almost peremptory tone in their demands for positive instructions and summary authority to arrest the evil. The suggestions of the writer were acknowledged by an appointment conferring upon himself the powers required for restoring order. The establishment of a permanent garrison under Colonel Wellesley's immediate command speedily brought the city to its ordinary state of tranquillity and confidence, and his services or his claims were still more conspicuously recognized by his subsequent nomination to the commission instituted for disposing of the conquered territories. Of these one portion was conferred on the Nizam, another offered to the Peishwa, a third retained by ourselves under the provisional government of Colonel Wellesley himself, and the remainder restored to the original proprietors, dispossessed by the usurpation of Tippoo and his father. In these hands it still remains, and the residence of the Court having been again transferred to its ancient capital, Mysore, Seringapatam, the creation of Hyder and Tippoo, and the scene of British triumphs, is now crumbling to ruins from desertion and neglect, and will probably leave as little visible trace as the dynasty which raised it. Such was the end of the famous war in which Arthur Wellesley first won consideration and renown. It is not easy, perhaps, at this period of time to appreciate the extraordinary interest with which it was viewed by contemporary observers, but it deserves to be remarked that these impressions were by no means confined to the shores of Britain. In the negotiations for the peace of Amiens the French plenipotentiaries repeatedly specified the conquest of Mysore as counterbalancing the continental triumphs of Napoleon himself, and the argument was acknowledged by Mr. Fox and his party to be founded on substantial reason.

We have now, within little more than two years of Colonel Wellesley's first landing at Calcutta, accompanied his rising fortunes to the point of independent and almost viceregal command. In July, 1799, he was actual Governor of Seringapatam and Mysore,—that is to say, of territories nearly equivalent to Tippoo's late kingdom; and as General Harris, on returning to the Presidency, had, in obedience to orders, surrendered to him the command in chief of the army of occupation, the civil and military authorities were united in his single person. The use which he made of these discretionary powers, and the account to which he turned such extraordinary opportunities of developing, correcting, and maturing his natural talents for organization and command, may be readily conceived. For some months he was now actively engaged in reconstituting the various departments of an Administration wholly disorganized by the overthrow of its chief; he selected and appointed officers in every capacity, giving preference to those who had faithfully discharged their duties under the former *régime;* he repaired roads, opened communications, attended to the claims of every class of the population, and executed with admirable sagacity all the functions of a Governor. Of the assiduity and talents which he brought to the performance of his duties his correspondence during this period with Colonel Close, the Resident at Mysore, contains copious illustration; but his services were soon to be again demanded in that capacity which was more peculiarly and memorably his own.

It is a characteristic of Oriental life that a few deeds of daring and a few turns of fortune will suffice to convert a freebooting adventurer into a popular captain, a mighty chief, and a recognised sovereign. Hyder Ali himself had been little more, and the existing rights of some princes of India are derived from a similar title. Scarcely had Tippoo's standard been overthrown when it was raised again by a rival, who, but for the opportune antagonism of Wellesley, might have repeated on a larger scale the pretensions and aggressions of the Mysorean usurper. The name of this desperado was Dhoondiah Waugh. Having been unable, even during Tippoo's life, to restrain his predatory propensities, he had been incarcerated in Seringapatam, and was only released at the general deliverance which attended our conquest of the capital. On escaping from his dungeon he betook himself to the district of Bednore, on the Mahratta frontier, collected a numerous force from the disbanded levies of the Sultaun, and proceeded to lay the country under contribution after the usual fashion of such aspirants. On being pursued by a British detachment he crossed the frontier, and ensconced himself in a territory which it was then thought very undesirable to violate. Just at this conjuncture Colonel Wellesley received an offer which might have exercised considerable influence on his subsequent career. It had been resolved to attempt, though by negotiation rather than force, the reduction of the Dutch settlement at Batavia, and the military command of the expedition was placed by Lord Mornington at the disposal of his brother. As the appointment was eventually declined, little notice would have been due to the incident but for the indirect testimonies which it elicited to Colonel Wellesley's services. Lord Clive, then Governor of Madras, dissuaded, in emphatic terms, the removal of a commander so indispensable to the peace of the Presidency, and Colonel Close alludes to the mere report of the project with expressions of unfeigned alarm. Wellesley himself remitted the question to the judgment of Lord Clive, not concealing his appreciation of the opportunity, but resolutely postponing all other considerations to those of the public service, and candidly avowing that Dhoondiah's progress was taking a very serious turn indeed. His disinterestedness on this occasion suggested the most advantageous policy he could possibly have adopted, for if Dhoondiah, whose fortunes were watched by a far more powerful foe, had been permitted to gather strength, either our Indian empire must have been crushed in its infancy, or the glories of the Mahratta war must have been gathered by other hands than those of Wellesley.

In point of fact, at the moment of writing the despatches with his conclusions on this critical subject, Colonel Wellesley was in the field on Dhoondiah's track. Towards the end of May he had put his troops in motion against this rapacious marauder, who, having assumed the title of "King of the Two Worlds," had appeared in imposing force on the borders of Mysore, alarming the well affected, enlisting the malcontents, and ravaging the whole country before him. There was, indeed, little likelihood that he would affect to make head against Colonel Wellesley's force in open field, but his troops were almost wholly composed of light cavalry and artillery, extremely difficult to overtake, and the seat of war, which was the "Dooab," or space between two rivers called the Kistnah and Toombudra, was peculiarly calculated to facilitate his plans. The country was intersected in all directions by rivers, which swelled prodigiously after rains, it was under no regular government, and had been exhausted by Dhoondiah's previous ravages. The exertions, therefore, of Colonel Wellesley in this, the first campaign which he ever directed in person, were turned to the means of concentrating his detachments in this difficult region, of provisioning his troops, and of either "running down" his adversary by rapid movements, or surprising him by adroit manœuvres. A subject of extreme importance was the disposition likely to be entertained at the Mahratta Court of Poohah, since the instructions of the British commander now empowered him to cross the frontier, if necessary, in pursuit of his antagonist—a step which he foresaw might entail a Mahratta war. The Peishwa, however, professed his readiness to co-operate in the campaign, but his contingent was routed by Dhoondiah with such promptitude, that little positive service was experienced from our allies, who would, there was little doubt, have declared against us on any of those reverses rendered so probable by the difficulties of the campaign. For several weeks Dhoondiah, by doubling and countermarching, succeeded in eluding his pursuers, and it seemed doubtful how long the expedition might be protracted, when Colonel Wellesley received an offer from a native to terminate the whole business by a stroke of a poniard. His reply was as follows:—"To offer a public reward by proclamation for a man's life, and to make a secret bargain to have it taken away, are two different things; the one is to be done; the other, in my opinion, cannot, by an officer at the head of his troops." The contest was continued, therefore, on even terms. More than once did the British commander succeed in driving his adversary into a position from which there appeared no escape, but as often did the wily freebooter defeat the imperfect vigilance of our allies, or avail himself of some unforeseen opportunity for eluding his pursuers. At length, on the 10th of September, 1800, after two months of a campaign in which he had extemporized from his own resources all the means of the commissariat and engineer department, and had subsisted his army almost by his own skill, Colonel Wellesley came upon the camp of his enemy. Though the whole force with him at that moment consisted but of four regiments of cavalry, harassed and overworked by constant marching, he at once "made a dash" at his prey, and put his army to the rout by a single charge, in encountering which Dhoondiah fell. The corpse of "his Majesty" being recognized, was lashed to a galloper gun and carried back to the British camp, but a certain item of the spoil deserves more particular mention. Among the baggage was found a boy about four years old, who proved to be the favourite son of Dhoondiah. Colonel Wellesley took charge of the child himself, carried him to his own tent, protected him through his boyhood, and, on quitting India, left a sum of money in the hands of a friend to be applied to his use.

This little war, if such a term can be applied to any hostilities in a country like India, was a simple rehearsal, both in character and result, of the great expeditions which were to follow. Against any antagonist but Wellesley it is highly probable that Dhoondiah's audacity and enterprise might have established him in a dominion equal to that of the Mahratta chiefs, whose power, indeed, had risen from an origin not dissimilar. At this moment the authority of the Peishwa was clearly on the decline, and threatened speedily to fall to the strongest, nor was there any reason why Dhoondiah should not have competed with Scindiah himself for the prize. The success of the recent campaign at once terminated all these risks, and confirmed Colonel Wellesley in an extraordinary reputation both with the native Courts and the British Government. The former were peculiarly qualified to appreciate such a victory as he had recently achieved, and the latter could not withhold their testimonies to the abilities by which the brother of the Governor-General had justified the appointments conferred upon him. In fact, though still a simple colonel, Arthur Wellesley was already, as he himself expressed it, "at the top of the tree," being intrusted with commissions above his rank, and honoured with the entire confidence of those whom he served. His attention, after the fall of Dhoondiah, had been directed under the ever present apprehension of Mahratta policy, to the Court of Poonah, but the jealousies subsisting between the Peishwa and his own feudatories, especially Scindiah, superseded for the moment any intrigues against the British dominion, and Colonel Wellesley was preparing to neutralize the ambition of the confederacy by supporting one of its members against the other, when events occurred which severely tested his moral fortitude, and which threatened at one time a serious interruption of his professional career.

It was in the autumn of the year 1800. Napoleon had struck down the powers of the continent, and was devising means for restoring to the French army in Egypt the resources they had lost by Nelson's victory of the Nile. In the eyes of Englishmen of those days, Egypt was always considered in the light of a high road to India; nor was it ever imagined that Napoleon's views in this direction could be bounded by the Red Sea. When, therefore, the force under Sir Ralph Abercromby was despatched to counterbalance the anticipated expedition of Napoleon, a scheme was conceived of making India contribute to its own security, by taking the French in rear, while Abercromby's army attacked them in front. In pursuance of this remarkable plan, originally suggested, we believe, by the Marquis Wellesley himself, a force, composed of detachments from the Indian armies, was to sail westward, to rendezvous at Mocha, to proceed thence to Cosseir, and to carry their co-operation across the Desert to the scene of war. The conception was actually executed; but so serious were the delays, in an enterprise without precedent or parallel, that the expedition only arrived at Cairo on the 10th of August, 1801, three months after the capitulation of General Belliard at that city had extinguished the prospects of the French in Egypt. With the expedition itself, therefore, not only as having been superfluous, but as not having included Colonel Wellesley among the officers employed, our present subject has little concern; but the circumstances attending its execution touched the fortunes of the future hero in some critical points, and served to display his constitutional qualities in a very instructive degree.

We have mentioned that among the expeditions projected by the Indian Government was one directed against Batavia. On the intelligence of Napoleon's demonstrations against our eastern possessions this scheme was abandoned, and it was resolved to substitute operations more immediately calculated to impede the advances of the French. With these views, a force of about 5,000 troops was collected at Trincomalee, in Ceylon, not with any fixed destination, but for the purpose of being thrown on such points as might be considered most advisable. Of this force Colonel Wellesley received the command, and he repaired accordingly to Trincomalee, from the theatre of his recent services in

Mysore. At the time of his arrival it was thought that the Mauritius offered the most promising point of attack; but the young commander soon discovered reasons for discarding this opinion, and had communicated his conclusions to the Governor-General, when he received intelligence which he permitted to decided his movements at once. A despatch from the home government had been forwarded to the Governor-General, directing the immediate preparation of the expedition mentioned above, and containing an authority for the prompt execution of the scheme, if circumstances should so advise, without waiting for instructions from Calcutta. A copy of this despatch had been left with the Governor of Madras, who transmitted it, without any directions of his own, to Colonel Wellesley at Trincomalee. The situation thus created was one of great delicacy and responsibility. Colonel Wellesley was convinced from the terms of the despatch that the expedition to Egypt must be immediately executed. He was perfectly aware that the troops under his command formed the only force available for the service; and he also knew that the destination now specially ordered had been among those contemplated for his detachment. Before he could receive from Calcutta any instructions founded on the despatch, four or five precious weeks would be sacrificed, and the aid of the expiring monsoon would be lost to his voyage. On the other hand, it required extraordinary confidence to assume so important a command, and to anticipate the orders of Government on a point of such serious magnitude. Colonel Wellesley's decision was characteristic. Relying, perhaps, partly on his brother's good opinion, but mainly, as we may fairly conceive, on the zeal for the service which had evidently prompted the resolution, he issued the necessary orders of his own authority, and set sail with the force under his command for the shores of the Red Sea. Learning, however, from the naval officers that the voyage would not be materially protracted by touching at Bombay, he resolved on adopting that course, for the double purpose of revictualling the transports and of receiving overland orders from the Governor-General, to whom he had immediately forwarded a statement of his intentions. On his arrival at Bombay he had the mortification to find his proceedings condemned, and himself superseded in his command.

From the light now thrown upon this subject by the Duke's despatches, we can perceive that the Governor-General, though privately acknowledging the substantial wisdom of his brother's decision, conceived that the general effect of the precedent, if uncensured, would more than counterbalance the advantages directly derivable, on any recurrence of a similar exigency. The actual supercession, however, of Colonel Wellesley, was not intended to carry a penal character. The Governor General had concluded, with obvious reason, that a command so important as the projected expedition involved should be given to a general officer, and he had, in fact, already selected General Baird for the appointment, while still under the impression that the troops were at Trincomalee, and that Batavia would be their fittest destination. In these conclusions it is not difficult to hold with the Governor-General; but, on the other hand, Colonel Wellesley argued that the decision on the point of standing required in the commanding officer should have been taken at the first notification of the appointment; that he had been publicly intrusted with the command in question, although it was thought possible that Egypt might be the destination of the expedition; that he had been recalled for this purpose from a lucrative and honourable commission in Mysore; and that to supersede him without cause given by his own default was seriously to injure his reputation and prospects. His behaviour under these circumstances was highly characteristic and exemplary. Lord Mornington rightly considered that, apart from the good of the service, it concerned his brother's professional character that he should not be positively excluded from an expedition of this active kind, and he therefore offered him the appointment of second in command to General Baird, at the same time leaving him the option of returning to his post in Mysore. The jealousies previously created between General Baird and Colonel Wellesley aggravated the unpleasantness of the affair, but under the obvious suggestions of the situation Colonel Wellesley had no doubts. He recorded his own annoyance, and his sense of the injustice he conceived himself to have suffered; but he remained at his post at Bombay, sent pledges of his cordial cooperation to General Baird, and, on hearing that the work had actually commenced in Egypt, prepared himself again to anticipate his superior officer by starting for the Red Sea without delay. "You will have seen," says he in a private letter to his brother Henry, "how much this resolution will annoy me, but I have never had much value for the public spirit of any man who does not sacrifice his private views and convenience when it is necessary." This was written on the 25th of March, 1801; but on the same evening Colonel Wellesley was seized with a fever at Bombay, and wholly disabled from embarking on the expedition at all. In this annoying conjuncture he addressed General Baird with great candour and generosity of sentiment, and enclosed him a memorandum on his operations in the Red Sea, evincing in a most remarkable degree the research and reflection he had expended on his anticipated command. These events, discouraging as they appeared, proved ultimately calculated, as the reader is aware, to develope even more signally than before the genius they seemed to repress. Colonel Wellesley returned to his command in Mysore, not for a service of inaction or routine, but to plan and conduct the operations of a war so extensive as to demand the highest efforts of professional skill, and so successful as to establish conclusively the supremacy of Britain in the East.

We delineated in a foregoing portion of this memoir the nature and extent of the empire or confederacy of the Mahrattas, which now constituted the only power from which the British Government had anything to dread. Though no permanent tranquillity was ever to have been anticipated by the side of these formidable rivals, yet so averse were the British authorities to war, and so eager to maintain the peace conducive to mercantile prosperity, that the Governor-General would willingly have retarded to the utmost the inevitable rupture, had not circumstances clearly demonstrated the expediency of immediate action. Independently of the apprehensions created by their immense resources and their inveterate aggressiveness, the Mahrattas were evoking at this moment the dreaded vision of French influence and ascendency. Though the peace of Amiens had checked the overt operations of our redoubtable rivals, their intrigues were continued with characteristic tenacity. Napoleon had sent Decaen to India with strict injunctions to provide for war while observing the stipulations of peace. Nor was this all; for Perron, a French adventurer, who had arrived in Hindostan twenty years previously, as a petty officer in Suffrein's squadron, was rising rapidly to the command of the whole Mahratta forces. He had disciplined and armed some 15,000 or 20,000 men for Scindiah's service, who were officered by his own countrymen, and who were not inferior to the trained battalions of the Company. His influence with Scindiah was so unbounded as actually to excite jealousy among the Mahratta chiefs; and if he had possessed the national spirit of Dupleix, or been opposed by any less a soldier than Arthur Wellesley, it is not too much to conceive that our Eastern empire might have hung upon a thread. So formidable even of itself was the Mahratta power, that nothing but the fortunate antagonism of the Affghans could have saved us from a rivalry which, in the infancy of our dominion, must have been fatal, and such an imposing mass of strength was now constituted by this addition of European discipline, that we may well rejoice in the destiny which reserved the struggle for the hero of Assaye.

Beyond the probabilities inseparable from Oriental policy, there was no reason for presuming that the several chiefs of the Mahratta nation had concerted any designs against the British Government. At that moment their intrigues had found a more immediate object in the headship of their own confederacy. The Peishwa—their nominal lord—was rapidly losing the power which had been usurped from the original sovereigns, and three of his sons, great feudatories, were preparing to contest his place. The Guicowar, having more to fear than to hope from his brethren, had permitted himself to be detached from their councils into an alliance with ourselves, which has subsisted to the present day; but Scindiah, Holkar, and the Berar Rajah were all resolute competitors for the supreme seat at Poonah. From these circumstances the British Government drew both the motives and means of action. The most powerful candidate was Scindiah, whose success, as we have shown above, would have virtually resulted in the establishment of French influence on a most formidable scale. This consummation, therefore, was, if possible, to be averted, and the Governor-General hoped that by conceding to the Peishwa that support which, in his weakness and peril, he had begged at our hands, and, by playing off against each other the mutual jealousies of his rivals, we might succeed, at least for a time, in obviating the dangers descried.

With these views a considerable force, under the command of General Stuart, was collected on the frontier of the Poonah territory, recently the scene of Dhoondiah's exploits. This was to serve the double purpose of demonstrating our strength, and protecting our own provinces, while a detachment about 7000 strong was to enter the dominions of the Peishwa for more active co-operation with that prince. It was in November, 1802, that Major-General Wellesley (for such, since April previous, had been his rank) received intelligence that an army was to be collected at the point in question. He had then been for eighteen months unobtrusively but vigorously engaged in the government of Mysore, to which, as we saw, he returned after being disappointed of his Egyptian command. The results of his administration were immediately conspicuous in the facilities of communication and unexampled copiousness of his supplies. The resources of Madras were outdone by the productiveness of Mysore. Though not yet aware that the direction of active operations was to devolve upon himself, his exertions were unremitting, and the interest he instinctively felt in the expedition will be seen in a remarkable journal which he kept of his daily proceedings, and which is published in the first volume of his despatches. So involuntarily was he engrossed by the idea of the campaign, that he even sketched out a plan of action for the benefit of the officer who might be employed. In point of fact, however, there could be but one opinion on this point. Whatever might be the reluctance entertained to part with General Wellesley from Mysore, or whatever the jealousies suggested by his rapid rise, it was perfectly undeniable that he, not only from his military talents, but from the peculiar knowledge he had acquired, both of the country and of the enemy with which we had to deal, was marked out for the appointment in question. He received it accordingly, in February, 1803, and, as his commission was extended four months afterwards to the supreme military and political charge of British affairs on the scene of operations, he found himself now invested with a command almost as responsible as those which he was afterwards to hold in Europe.

There was, as we observed, no declaration of war at this moment between the Mahrattas and the British, nor was the force of the detachment originally sent into the Peishwa's territory in any degree measured by the known resources of the Mahratta chiefs, although their open hostility was a matter of probable occurrence. The immediate object of General Wellesley was to protect the Peishwa from summary dethronement, a result which he accomplished by a skilful and rapid movement upon Poonah. After the establishment of the legitimate authority by this open demonstration of British alliance, and by the encouragement of well-disposed vassals, the proceedings of the British were to be regulated by the attitude of the refractory chiefs; and this attitude grew daily so menacing, that the Governor-General resolved to attempt his ulterior objects of dispersing M. Perron's battalions and circumscribing the enormous pretensions of Scindiah. Accordingly, while Lake took the field in Hindostan for the memorable campaign of Laswarree, General Wellesley was invested, as we have said, with full powers to commence active operations against the Mahratta forces in the Deccan. The force at his command for these purposes consisted of about 10,000 men of all arms, Europeans and natives, including the 19th dragoons, and the 74th regiment of foot. He had desired that his old corps, the 33d, should be attached to his division, but circumstances prevented the arrangement. The duty of co-operating with his movements devolved on Colonel Stevenson, an excellent officer, who commanded for this purpose the subsidiary force of the Nizam, which, by the addition of the 94th regiment, had been raised to about the same strength as General Wellesley's division.

In the ensuing campaign General Wellesley's duties consisted in so combining his movements that none of his detachments were taken at a disadvantage, that the peculiar qualities of the British troops might be turned to the best account, and that the difficulties of Indian warfare might be obviated by wary provision, or surmounted by vigorous enterprise. It was now that his contemporaries had the opportunity of observing his singular faculties of foresight and his extraordinary aptitude in all departments of his profession. In his affair with Dhoondiah he had accurately noted the characteristics of native warfare, the chief features and serviceable points of the country, the strength of the forts, and the course, depth, and periodical variations of the rivers. From these observations he had conceived his plans of a Mahratta campaign. Selecting a season when the rivers were not fordable, he turned this feature of the country to the advantage of the British by preparing boats and pontoons, with which he knew the enemy would be unprovided. His despatches contain the most minute instructions for the fabrication of these bridges and boats, for the establishment of particular ferries, and for their protection by proper guards. Aware that a native army relied on the superior rapidity of its movements, he had been indefatigable in improving the breed of draught-bullocks by the aid of Tippoo's famous stock; and he had resolved, when occasion came, to discard the traditional rules of marching and halting. The forts, he observed, were strong enough, if well defended, to give serious trouble, and too numerous to be besieged in form. He gave orders, therefore, by way of conveying an adequate idea of British prowess, that one or two of them should be carried by simple escalade, and that an example should be made of the garrison in case of any desperate resistance. These tactics were completely successful. A Mahratta chief wrote to his friend as follows :—" These English are a strange people, and their general a wonderful man. They came in here this morning, looked at the Pettah wall, walked over it, killed all the garrison, and returned to breakfast. Who can withstand them ?" The result was that the strongest forts in the country were afterwards taken with little or no loss of life on either side.

Meantime the demonstrations of the great Mahratta chiefs grew more and more overtly hostile. For the main body of Scindiah's troops Lake was finding ample work between Delhi and Agra, but a force including 10,000 of his disciplined infantry was hovering over the Deccan; Holkar, though he had hitherto retired before the British, was known to be dangerous, and the Rajah of Berar was more than suspected of sharing their common views. The object, therefore, was first to compel these chieftains to an avowal of their intentions, and next, in the event of the probable result, to bring them to a decisive action. The plenary authority which General Wellesley received on the 26th of June enabled him to cut short the negotiations which had been purposely protracted, and to reduce Scindiah to his proper character. After some wearisome manœuvres he at length learnt that the enemy was on the north bank of the Godavery, meditating a swoop on Hyderabad. "If the river," he now wrote, "does not become fordable six weeks sooner than usual, I hope to strike a blow against their myriads of horse in a few days." This was on the 30th of August. On the 21st of September, having received more particular information, he concerted measures with Colonel Stevenson that one should take a western route and the other an eastern, and both fall together from opposite quarters on the enemy's camp early on the 24th. The next day the two divisions diverged accordingly, and pursued their respective routes, when on the 23d General Wellesley learnt from his spies that the Mahratta cavalry had moved off, but that the infantry were still encamped at about six miles distance. Pushing on with his dragoons he presently descried not only the infantry, but the entire army of the Mahrattas in the Deccan, numbering at least 50,000 combatants, and strongly posted, with 100 pieces of cannon before the fortified village of ASSAYE.

At this critical moment of his fortunes the force which General Wellesley had in hand, including the infantry which was coming up, did not exceed 4,500 men; his few light guns were utterly unable to make head against the tremendous batteries of the Mahrattas, and his draught cattle, notwithstanding the pains he had expended on them, were sinking under the severity of the campaign. His resolution, however, was taken at once, and without measuring the relative proportion of the two armies, or waiting for Colonel Stevenson to share the perils and glories of the field, he gave instant orders for the attack. Owing to a misapprehension of instructions, his precautionary directions for avoiding the most menacing points of the Mahratta position were disregarded, and the battle was won with a terrible carnage with the bayonet alone, exactly like some of the actions recently witnessed with the Sikhs. But nothing could be more decisive than the victory obtained, which not only at once brought Scindiah to terms, but served, in the estimation of competent judges, to proclaim beyond reach of further challenge the military supremacy of the British. Taught by our example, and the aid of European officers, the natives had gradually brought their armies to an apparent equality with our own. The cumbrous and ill-served artillery trains, the unwieldy masses and irregular hordes of our early antagonists, had now given place to disciplined battalions formed of the same material as those of the Company, and to batteries of deadly strength, manned by skilful and devoted gunners. It now remained to be seen whether the success of the British arms depended on any element inaccessible to native emulation, and this enigma was solved, once and for all, by Wellesley at Assaye. With forces almost as numerically disproportionate as those of Clive, he had surpassed the glories of Arcot and Plassey against an enemy far more formidable than Chunda Sahib, or Suraj-a-Dowlah. With all odds but those of science and spirit against him, he had maintained and confirmed the *prestige* superstitiously attached to the arms of England, and to this, the first pitched battle in which he ever commanded, has been plausibly traced the establishment of that ascendency which we enjoy in India to this very day.

Though it was clear, both to British and Mahrattas, that the whole campaign was virtually decided by such a triumph as that of Assaye, yet the native chiefs, who, as Wellesley on this occasion described them, were "rashness personified," evinced resolutions of provoking yet another battle. Scindiah, it is true, under the combined teaching of Wellesley and Lake, had received a lesson which, to the latest days of his life, he never forgot; but the Rajah of Berar was still in the field, and as General Wellesley two months afterwards was on the Mahratta track to compel adherence to the covenanted stipulations, and to clear the country of any dangerous gatherings, he came one evening upon the whole remaining force of the enemy, drawn up in battle array before the village of Argaum, to renew again the experiment of September. Considering that since the last battle the British had been strengthened almost as much as they themselves had been weakened, it was a forlorn hazard, yet a body of Persian cavalry in the Berar service made a desperate charge on the European regiments, and Scindiah's horsemen, who, notwithstanding the recent treaty, were found in the ranks of our adversaries, made a show of supporting the attack. The advance of the British line, however, was not waited for by the main body of the Mahrattas, who in the hopeless confusion abandoned their guns and fled, but only to fall, through the long hours of a moonlight night, under the sabres of their pursuers.

With these operations, the capture of some strongholds, and the surprise and destruction of a new competitor for Dhoondiah's fame, ended our first Mahratta war, in which, owing to the genius and energy of our generals, we had prostrated, with incredible rapidity, that redoubtable foe whose enmity had been for years the traditional dread of the Indian Government. The personal contributions of Wellesley towards this consummation were well appreciated by those most intimately concerned. The British inhabitants of Calcutta voted him a valuable sword, the native population of Seringapatam received him with unfeigned congratulations on his return, and upon his departure from India, which soon followed, the thanks, the addresses, and the offerings of civilians, soldiers, and presidencies poured upon him in quick succession. A yet more remarkable testimony to the value of his services may be gathered from the opinions of that mighty antagonist with whom, at a future day, he was to compete in deadly grapple for the championship of the world. While Wellesley was clearing the Deccan of England's last enemies, Napoleon was mustering the whole resources of his empire on the heights of Boulogne for a descent on the island of his hate. The flotilla was ready, the camps were formed, and the conveying squadron anxiously expected from the west, when, at this very moment, with a vision of conquest before his eyes, he wavered, as we are now told by his latest biographer, for some weeks together, between the ideas of destroying us by invasion or attacking us through the side of India by reviving the Mahratta war!

It was in the month of September, 1805, that Sir Arthur Wellesley—after an absence of nine years, during which his services in the East had earned him a Major-Generalship, the Knighthood of the Bath, the thanks of the King and Parliament, and a confirmed professional reputation—landed once more on the shores of England. Between this period and his departure on those memorable campaigns with which his name will be immortally connected there elapsed an interval in the Duke's life of nearly three years, which a seat in Parliament, an Irish Secretaryship, and a Privy Councillorship enabled him to turn actively to account. His proper talents, however, were not overlooked, and he bore his part in those notable "expeditions" which were then conceived to measure the military power of England. His arrival from India had exactly coincided with the renewal of the war against France by the third European coalition—a compact to which England was a party. Our specific duties in these alliances were usually limited to the supply of ships and money. We swept the ocean with our fleets, and we subsidized the great Powers whose forces were actually in the field. As to the British army itself, that had been hitherto reckoned among the contingents of second and third-rate States, which might be united perhaps for a convenient diversion, but which could make no pretension to service in the great European line of battle. At the beginning of the war these demonstrations had usually been made on the coasts of France, but they were now principally directed against the northern and southern extremities of the Continent, and for these reasons:—the dominion, actual or confessed, of Napoleon, against which the contest was undertaken, embraced all the ports of Europe, from the Texel to Genoa, while his battle array extended along the length of the Rhine. The masses, therefore, of the Austrian and Russian hosts were moved directly against

France from the east, and to the minor allies was left the charge of penetrating either upwards from Naples, or downwards from Swedism Pomerania, to the theatre of action. Sometimes detachments from Gibraltar and Malta disembarked in Italy in conjunction with Russians from Corfu and Neapolitans from Calabria, and sometimes we landed in Hanover to compose a joint stock force with Swedes, Norwegians, and Finlanders. One of these latter expeditions fell to the lot of Sir Arthur Wellesley immediately after his return, but with results even fewer than usual. The brigades were put on shore at Bremen at the close of 1805; but Napoleon in the meantime had done his work so effectually on the Danube that our contingent returned to England after a few weeks' absence without striking a blow. Sir Arthur's next service was one of greater distinction. In 1807, when the British Ministry had boldly determined upon anticipating Napoleon at Copenhagen by one of his own strokes of policy, the feelings of the Danes were consulted by the despatch of a force so powerful as to justify a bloodless capitulation, and in this army Sir Arthur Wellesley received a command which brought under his charge the chief military operation of the expedition. While the main body was menacing Copenhagen a demonstration was observed on the part of the Danes against the English rear, and Sir Arthur was detached to disperse their gathering battalions. This service he effectually performed by engaging them in their position of Kioge, and putting them to the rout with the loss of 1,500 prisoners and 14 pieces of cannon. He was afterwards intrusted with the negotiations for the capitulation of the city—

a duty which was skilfully discharged. This short episode in his military life has been thrown into shadow by his mightier achievements; but its merits were acknowledged by the special thanks of Parliament; and M. Thiers, in his history, introduces Sir Arthur Wellesley to French readers as an officer who had certainly seen service in India, but who was principally known by his able conduct at Copenhagen.

At length, at the very moment when England seemed to be excluded from all participation in the military contests of the age, and the services of the British soldier appeared likely to be measured by the demands of colonial duty, events brought an opportunity to pass which ultimately resulted in one of the most memorable wars on record, and enabled Britain to support a glorious part in what, without figure of rhetoric, we may term the liberation of Europe. The coalition effected against France at the period of Sir Arthur Wellesley's return had been scattered to the winds under the blows of Napoleon. Russia had been partly driven and partly inveigled into a concert of politics with her redoubtable adversary; Austria had been put *hors de combat*, and Prussia was helplessly prostrate. To complete the concern experienced at this prospect of universal dominion Napoleon had availed himself of the occasion to seize and appropriate the whole of the Spanish Peninsula. Under the pretence of a treaty with Spain for the partition of Portugal he had poured his troops into the former country, overrun the latter, and then repudiated the stipulations of his compact by retaining undivided possession of the prize. A few months later he established himself in a similar authority at Madrid, and made open avowal of his intentions by bestowing on his own brother the inheritance of the Spanish Bourbons. Scarcely, however, had his projects been disclosed when he encountered a tempest of popular opposition; the nations of the Peninsula rose almost as one man; a French army was compelled to capitulate, King Joseph decamped from Madrid, and Marshal Junot was with difficulty enabled to maintain himself in Lisbon. At the intelligence of this unexpected display of vigour England tendered her substantial sympathies to the Spanish patriots; the overtures of their juntas were favourably received, and at length it was decided by the Portland Ministry that Portugal would be as good a point as any other on which to throw 10,000 troops, who were waiting at Cork for embarcation on the next "expedition" suggesting itself. Such was the origin of the Peninsular War—an enterprise at first considered, and even for some time afterwards reputed, as importing little more to the interests or renown of the nation than a diversion at Stralsund or Otranto, but which now, enshrined in the pages of a famous history and viewed by the light of experience, will take its place among the most memorable contests which the annals of Europe record. Beyond doubt, the enthusiasm of the British nation at this conjuncture was unusually great, and there were not wanting arguments to prove that the contemplated expedition differed greatly in its promise from those heretofore recommended to favour. It was urged that Napoleon was now for the first time encountered by strong popular opinion, and that the scene of action, moreover, was a sea-girt territory, giving full scope for the exercise of our naval supremacy. These observations were sound, but it must needs have been expected by many that the "particular service" now announced to the nation would have the ordinary termination, and that the transports bound for Portugal would soon return, as others had returned before them from St. Domingo and the Helder, from Quiberon Bay and Ferrol. Nor was it owing, indeed, either to the wisdom of the nation or the strength of the cause that such predictions were belied by the triumphs and glories of an immortal war.

To comprehend the service now intrusted to Sir A. Wellesley it will be necessary to retain constantly in mind the circumstances and persuasions under which it was undertaken. The actual state of the countries which it was proposed to succour was only known from the exaggerated descriptions of the Spanish patriots, who represented themselves as irresistible in military strength, and as needing nothing but stores and money to expel the French from the Peninsula. Nothing was ascertained respecting Napoleon's actual force in these parts; and, although it might reasonably have been inferred, from the continental peace, that the whole hosts of the French Empire were disposable on the one side, and, from the contradictory reports of the Spanish envoys themselves, that neither unity nor intelligence existed on the other, these simple deductions were not drawn. The British Ministry had despatched the expedition without any purpose more definite than that of aiding in the resistance unexpectedly offered to France on the Peninsular territories. It had not been determined whether the landing should be effected in

Portugal or Spain, and, with the latter country, indeed, we were nominally at war when the armament was decreed. Neither was the single appointment which compensated all these deficiencies the result of any general or deliberate convictions. The nomination of Sir Arthur Wellesley to the command was chiefly due to the individual sagacity of Lord Castlereagh, whose judgment on this point was considerably in advance of that of other and higher authorities. Even this appointment itself, too, was intended to be nugatory, for Sir Arthur was to surrender the command to Sir Harry Burrard, who was in turn to make way for Sir Hew Dalrymple, and in the form which the expedition shortly afterwards assumed no fewer than six general officers were placed above him, into whose hands the conduct of the war was ultimately to fall.

True, however, to that spirit of his profession which forbade him to balance his own feelings against the good of the service or the decisions of the Government, Sir Arthur departed on his mission, preceding the expeditionary armament in a fast frigate, for the purpose of obtaining more information than was already possessed respecting the destination to be given to it. With these views he landed on the coast, and conferred with the juntas directing the affairs of the insurrection. His inquiries soon proved conclusive if not satisfactory, and he decided with characteristic penetration, that "it was impossible to learn the truth." In point of fact, at the moment when the expedition was hovering irresolutely between the Douro and the Tagus—that is to say at the conclusion of July, 1808—the Spaniards had really experienced extraordinary success at Baylen ;

but this victory was unknown to those who vaunted to Sir Arthur the magnitude of their forces, and whose ignorant vain-gloriousness was instantly detected by his acute and impartial vision. Dupont had been circumvented in the south, but the other French Generals had been easily victorious in the north, and a force was at hand under Napoleon sufficient to sweep the country between the Pyrenees and Madrid. The patriot levies were miserably destitute of equipments and discipline, and below their reported strength even in mere numbers; their rulers were mostly devoid of any better qualities for the contest than national obstinacy and thoroughgoing hate, while as to unity of purpose or organization of means there were no such features visible in any quarter of the Peninsula. Portugal offered somewhat better opportunities. Its geographical position favoured the designs of the English commander, and its internal conditions offered considerable inducements to a descent on these parts. Junot, cut off from all communication with his colleagues in the Peninsula, was maintaining his ground with difficulty at Lisbon between the insurgents of Portugal and the menacing patriots of Spain. The troops under his command amounted to fully 25,000 men, but so many detachments were required for various services that his disposable force could only become formidable by virtue of greater military skill than he happened to possess. He himself lay with a large garrison at Lisbon, and on the first rumours of the British expedition he despatched General Loison with a movable column of some 7,000 men, to scour the country, overwhelm the insurrection, and "drive the English into the sea."

After ascertaining and estimating these prospects to the best of his power, Sir Arthur Wellesley decided on the disembarking his troops in Mondego Bay, about midway between Oporto and Lisbon — a resolution which he successfully executed at the beginning of August. The force actually landed from the transports amounted to about 9,000 men; but they were presently joined by that of another little expedition which had been operating in the south of Spain, and Sir Arthur thus found himself at the head of some 14,000 excellent soldiers. Besides these, however, the British Government, as the design of liberating the Peninsula gradually assumed substance and dignity, determined on despatching two others of their corps-errant, one of which, nearly 12,000 strong, under Sir John Moore, was in a state of discipline not inferior to that of Napoleon's best brigades. 30,000 troops, therefore, were eventually to represent the arms of England in this memorable service; but wisdom had to be learnt before Wellesley was placed at their head, and it was with 13,000 only, and a provisional command, that the great captain of the age commenced on the 9th of August his first march in the Peninsular War.

The intention of Sir Arthur, who in the absence of his two seniors still retained the direction of affairs, was to march on Lisbon by the seacoast, in order to draw from the English store-ships in the offing those supplies which he had already discovered it was hopeless to expect from the resources of Portugal itself; one of the earliest propositions of the Portuguese commander having suggested that his own troops should be fed from the British commissariat instead of the British troops from his. Reinforced, if the term can be used, at this period with a small detachment of the native army, Sir Arthur now mustered nearly 15,000 sabres and bayonets. To oppose him, Loison had about 7,000 men, Laborde about 5,000, and Junot, at headquarters, some 10,000 more. Of these commanders Loison was on the left of the British route, and Laborde in front; nor was Sir Arthur's information accurate enough to enable him to estimate the point or period of their probable junction. As events turned out, his military instinct had divined the course proper to be pursued, for by pressing forward on Laborde he interposed himself between this general and Loison, and encountered his enemies in detail. Laborde's outposts at Ovidos were promptly driven in on the 15th, and on the 17th Sir Arthur came up with his antagonist on the heights of Roliça, and there gained the first action of the war. The engagement was sustained with great spirit; for Laborde, though outnumbered, availed himself to the utmost of his strength of position, nor was it without serious loss on both sides that he was at length compelled to retire. After this satisfactory essay of arms Sir Arthur prepared to meet Junot, who would, he was well aware, summon all his strength for the now inevitable encounter, and who had in fact concentrated 16,000 men with 21 guns at Torres Vedras, between Sir Arthur's position and Lisbon. Still moving by the coast, the British commander was fortunately reinforced on his march by one of the detachments despatched from home, as we before observed, to participate in the expedition, and his force was thus augmented to 18,000 effective men. With these means he proposed to turn

Junot's position at Torres Vedras by passing between it and the sea with his advanced guard, while the main body occupied the enemy's attention in front, so that the French general would either be cut off from Lisbon or driven to a precipitate retreat. These able dispositions, however, were not brought to the test of trial; for at this moment Sir Harry Burrard arrived off the coast, and, without quitting his ship or troubling himself to confirm by his own observation the representations of Sir Arthur, counter-ordered the proposed march, and gave directions for halting on the ground then occupied—the hills of Vimiera—until the arrival of the other and larger reinforcement expected from England under Sir John Moore.

Among the facts which Sir Arthur had laboured to impress on his intractable superior, was that of the certainty of immediately receiving the attack which he was declining to give—a conclusion which was promptly verified by the appearance of Junot in battle array the very next morning. The estimates, therefore, respectively formed by Sir Harry and Sir Arthur concerning the relative capacities of the two armies were presently to be certified by experience, and the decisive defeat of Junot at every point of his attack, with the loss of 3,000 men and nearly all his artillery, might have been thought decisive of the question in the eyes of impartial observers. Sir Harry, however, was still unconvinced, and, in his firm persuasion of the superiority of the French, refused the permission now earnestly entreated by Sir Arthur to intercept the encumbered brigades of the enemy, and complete his discomfiture by cutting off his retreat to Torres Vedras.

It was on this occasion that Sir Arthur, seeing the sacrifice of an opportunity which might have been turned to the completion of the war, turned round and said to his staff—" Well, then, gentlemen, we may go now and shoot red-legged partridges."

No sooner had this supercession of Sir Arthur Wellesley occurred than a second change took place in the command of the English force, and the arrangements of the British Government were notably exemplified by the arrival on the scene of Sir Hew Dalrymple, who immediately displaced Sir Henry Burrard, as Sir Henry Burrard had displaced Sir Arthur Wellesley. Unfortunately, the new general inclined to the opinions of his second in command, rather than to the more enterprising tactics of the future hero of the Peninsula, and he persisted in the belief that Sir John Moore's corps should be allowed to come up before operations were recommenced. The best commentary on Sir Arthur's advice is to be found in the fact that Junot himself presently proposed a suspension of arms, with a view to the complete evacuation of Portugal by the French. A convention, in fact, was concluded on these terms, at Cintra, within a fortnight after the battle; but so adroitly had Junot and his comrades availed themselves of the impressions existing at the British head-quarters that, though beaten in the field, they maintained in the negotiations the ascendency of the stronger party, and eventually secured conditions far more favourable than they were entitled to demand. It happened that Sir Arthur Wellesley had been made, under Sir Hew Dalrymple's immediate orders, the negotiating officer at the first agreement between the belligerents, and it was his name which appeared at the foot of the instrument. When, therefore, the indignation of Englishmen was, with some justice, roused at this sacrifice of their triumphs, and the convention made the subject of official inquiry, General Wellesley incurred the first shock of public censure. Further investigation, however, not only exculpated him from all responsibility, but brought to light his earnest, though ineffectual endeavours, to procure a different result, and the country was soon satisfied that if the conqueror of Roliça and Vimiera had been undisturbed in his arrangements, the whole French army must have been prisoners of war. Yet, even as things stood, the success achieved was of no ordinary character. The British soldiers had measured their swords against some of the best troops of the Empire, and with signal success. The "Sepoy General" had indisputably shown that his powers were not limited to Oriental campaigns. He had effected the disembarcation of his troops—always a most hazardous feat—without loss, had gained two well contested battles; and in less than a single month had actually cleared the kingdom of Portugal of its invaders. The army, with its intuitive judgment, had formed a correct appreciation of his services, and the field-officers engaged at Vimiera testified their opinions of their commander by a valuable gift; but it was clear that no place remained for General Wellesley under his new superiors, and he accordingly returned to England, bringing with him conceptions of Spanish affairs which were but too speedily verified by events.

While Sir Arthur Wellesley, having resumed his Irish Secretaryship and his seat in Parliament, was occupying himself with the civil duties of his office, and endeavouring to promote a better comprehension of Peninsular politics, an abrupt change of fortune had wholly reversed the relative positions of the French and English in those parts. The successes of the summer and autumn had expelled Napoleon's forces from Portugal, and from nearly nine-tenths of the territory of Spain, the only ground still occupied by the invaders being a portion of the mountainous districts behind the Ebro. Thus, after sweeping the whole Peninsula before them by a single march, and establishing themselves at Madrid and Lisbon with less trouble than had been experienced at Brussels or Amsterdam, the French armies found themselves suddenly driven back, by a return tide of conquest, to the very foot of the Pyrenees; and now, in like manner, the English, after gaining possession of Portugal in a month's campaign, and closing round upon their enemies in Spain as if to complete the victory, were as suddenly hurled back again to the coast, while the Peninsula again passed apparently under the dominion of Napoleon, to be finally rescued by a struggle of tenfold severity. Sir Arthur Wellesley quitted Portugal towards the end of September, leaving behind him a British force of some 30,000 men, committed to an indefinite co-operation with the Spanish patriots. At this period the remains of the French armies of occupation were, as we have said, collected behind the Ebro, in number, perhaps, about 50,000 or 60,000, while the Spanish forces, in numerical strength at least double, were disposed around them in a wide semicircular cordon, from Bilbao to Barcelona; and it was conceived that an English army advancing from the west would at once give the finishing impulse to the campaign. But, in point of fact, these appearances were on both sides delusive. The Spanish armies were deficient in every point but that of individual enthusiasm. They were almost destitute of military provisions and were under no effective command. The administration of the country since the insurrection had been conducted by provincial juntas acting independently of each other, and, although an attempt had been made to centralize these powers by the organization of a supreme junta at Aranjuez, little success had as yet attended the experiment. The consequence was a total distraction of counsels, an utter confusion of government, and a general spirit of self-will and insubordination, which the recent successes only tended to increase. Such was the true condition of the patriot forces. On the other hand, the French, though repulsed for the moment, were close to the inexhaustible resources of their own country; and Napoleon, with a perfect appreciation of the scene before him, was preparing one of those decisive blows which none better than he knew how to deal. The army behind the Ebro had been rapidly reinforced to the amount of 150,000 men, and at the beginning of November the Emperor arrived in person to assume the command. At this conjuncture Sir John Moore, who, it will be remembered, had brought the last and largest detachment to the army of Portugal, and who had remained in that country while the other generals had repaired to England pending the inquiry into the convention of Cintra, was directed to take the command of 21,000 men from the army of Portugal, to unite with a corps of 7,000 more despatched to Corunna under Sir David Baird, and to co-operate with the Spanish forces beleaguering the French, as we have described, in the south-eastern angle of the Peninsula. In pursuance of these instructions, Sir John Moore, by a series of movements which we are not called upon in this place to criticise, succeeded in collecting at Salamanca by the end of November the troops under his own command, while Sir David Baird's corps had penetrated as far as Astorga. But the opportunity of favourable action, if ever it had really existed, was now past. Suddenly advancing with an imposing force of the finest troops of the empire, Napoleon had burst through the weak lines of his opponents, had crushed their armies to the right and left by a succession of irresistible blows, was scouring with his cavalry the plains of Leon and Castile, forced the Somosierra pass on the 30th of November, and four days afterwards was in undisputed possession of Madrid. Meantime Sir John Moore, misled by false intelligence, disturbed by the importunities of our own Minister at Aranjuez, disheartened by his observation of Spanish politics, and despairing of any substantial success against an enemy of whose strength he was now aware, determined, after long hesitation, on advancing into the country, with the hope of some advantage against the corps of Soult, isolated, as he thought, at Saldanha. The result of this movement was to bring Napoleon from Madrid in such force as to compel the rapid retreat of the English to Corunna under circumstances which we need not recount; and thus by the commencement of the year 1809, Spain was again occupied by the French, while the English army, so recently victorious in Portugal, was saving itself by sea without having struck a blow, except in self-defence at its embarcation.

Napoleon, before Moore's corps had actually left Corunna, conceived the war at an end, and, in issuing instructions to his marshals, anticipated, with no unreasonable confidence, the complete subjugation of the Peninsula. Excepting, indeed, some isolated districts in the south-east, the only parts now in possession of the Spaniards or their allies were Andalusia, which had been saved by the precipitate recall of Napoleon to the North, and Portugal, which, still in arms against the French, was nominally occupied by a British corps of 10,000 men, left there under Sir John Cradock at the time of General Moore's departure with the bulk of the army for Spain. The proceedings of the French marshals for the recovery of the entire Peninsula were speedily arranged. Lannes took the direction of the siege of Saragossa, where the Spaniards, fighting as usual with admirable constancy from behind stone walls, were holding two French corps at bay. Lefebvre drove one Spanish army into the recesses of the Sierra Morena, and Victor chased another into the fastnesses of Murcia. Meantime Soult, after recoiling awhile from the dying blows of Moore, had promptly occupied Gallicia after the departure of the English, and was preparing to cross the Portuguese frontier on his work of conquest. In aid of this design, it was concerted that while the last-named marshal advanced from the north, Victor, by way of Elvas, and Lapisse, by way of Almeida, should converge together upon Portugal, and that when the English at Lisbon had been driven to their ships, the several corps should unite for the final subjugation of the Peninsula, by the occupation of Andalusia. Accordingly, leaving Ney to maintain the ground already won, Soult descended with 30,000 men upon the Douro, and by the end of March was in secure possession of Oporto. Had he continued his advance, it is not impossible that the campaign might have had the termination he desired; but at this point, he waited for intelligence of the English in his front and of Victor and Lapisse on his flank. His caution saved Portugal, for, while he still hesitated on the brink of the Douro, there again arrived in the Tagus that renowned commander, before whose genius the fortunes not only of the marshals, but of their imperial master, were finally to fail.

England was now at the commencement of her greatest war. The system of small expeditions and insignificant diversions, though not yet conclusively abandoned, was soon superseded by the glories of a visible contest; and in a short time it was known and felt by a great majority of the nation, that on the field of the Peninsula England was fairly pitted against France, and playing her own chosen part in the European struggle. But these convictions were not prevalent enough at the outset to facilitate in any material degree the duties of the Ministry or the work of the General; on the contrary, so complicated were the embarrassments attending the prosecution of the war on the scale required, that to surmount them demanded little less wisdom or patience than the conduct of the actual campaign. In the first instance, the British nation had been extravagantly excited by the successful insurrections of the Spaniards, and the events of our experimental campaign in Portugal had so inspired the public mind, that even the evacuation of that kingdom by the French was considered, as we have seen, in the light of an imperfect result. When, however, these conditions of the struggle were rapidly exchanged for the total discomfiture of the patriots, the recapture of Madrid, and the precipitate retreat of the British army, with the loss of its commander, and the salvation of little but its honor, popular opinion veered quickly towards its customary point, and it was loudly proclaimed that the French Emperor was invincible by land, and that a contest with his legions on that element must inevitably prove ruinous to Britain. But the government of the day, originally receiving its impulse from public feeling, had gradually acquired independent convictions on this mighty question, and was now prepared to maintain the interests of the nation against the clamours of the nation itself. Accordingly, at the commencement of the year 1809, when the prospects of Spanish independence were at their very gloomiest point, the British Cabinet had proposed and concluded a comprehensive treaty of alliance with the Provisional Administration of Spain; and it was now resolved that the contest in the Peninsula should be continued on a scale more effectual than before, and that the principal, instead of the secondary, part should be borne by England. Yet this decision was not taken without much hesitation and considerable resistance; and it was clear to all observant spectators that, though the opinions of the Government, rather than those of the opposition, might preponderate in the public mind, their ascendency was not so complete but that the first incidents of failure, loss, or difficulty, would be turned to serious account against the promoters and conductors of the war.

Nor were these misgivings, though often pretended for the purpose of faction, without a certain warrant of truth; indeed, few can read the history of this struggle without perceiving that the single point which concluded it in our favour, was the genius of that great man who has just expired. It has been attempted to show that the military forces of France and England at this period were not in reality so disproportioned as they appeared to be, but we confess our own inability to discover the balance alleged. It is beyond doubt that the national spirit remained unchanged, and that the individual excellence of the British soldier was unimpeachable Much, too, had been done in the way of organization by the measures consequent on the protracted menace of invasion, and much in the way of encouragement by the successes in Egypt and Portugal no less than the triumphs in India. But in war numerical force must needs tell with enormous effect, and on this point England's colonial requirements left her little to show against the myriads of the continent. It was calculated at the time that 60,000 British soldiers *might* have been made disposable for the Peninsular service, but at no period of the war was such a force ever actually collected under the standards of Wellington, while Napoleon could maintain his 300,000 warriors in Spain, whithout disabling the arms of the Empire on the Danube or the Rhine. We had allies, it is true, in the troops of the country; but these at first were little better than refractory recruits, requiring all the accessories of discipline, equipment, and organization; jealous of all foreigners even as friends, and not unreasonably suspicious of supporters, who could always find in their ships a refuge which was denied to themselves. But above all these difficulties was that arising from the inexperience of the Government in continental warfare. Habituated to expeditions reducible to the compass of a few transports, unaccustomed to the contingencies of regular war, and harassed by a vigilant and not always conscientious Opposition, the Ministry had to consume half its strength at home; and the commander of the army, in justifying his most skilful dispositions, or procuring needful supplies for the troops under his charge, was driven to the very extremities of expostulation and remonstrance.

When, however, with these ambiguous prospects, the Government did at length resolve on the systematic prosecution of the Peninsular war, the eyes of the nation were at once instinctively turned on Sir Arthur Wellesley as the general to conduct it. Independently of the proofs he had already given of his quality at Roliça and Vimiera, this enterprising and sagacious soldier stood almost alone in his confidence respecting the undertaking on hand. Arguing from the military position of Portugal, as flanking the long territory of Spain, from the natural features of the country (which he had already studied), and from the means of reinforcement and retreat securely provided by the sea, he stoutly declared his opinion that Portugal was tenable against the French, even if actual possessors of Spain, and that it offered ample opportunities of influencing the great result of the war. With these views he recommended that the Portuguese army should be organized at its full strength; that it should be in part taken into British pay and under the direction of British officers, and that a force of not less than 30,000 English troops should be despatched to keep this army together. So provided, he undertook the management of the war, and such were his resources, his tenacity, and his skill, that though 280,000 French soldiers were closing round Portugal as he landed at Lisbon, and though difficulties of the most arduous kind awaited him in his task, he neither flinched nor failed until he had led his little army in triumph, not only from the Tagus to the Ebro, but across the Pyrenees into France, and returned himself by Calais to England after witnessing the downfall of the French capital.

Yet, so perilous was the conjuncture when the weight of affairs was thus thrown upon his shoulders, that a few weeks' more delay must have destroyed every prospect of success. Not only was Soult, as we stated, collecting himself for a swoop on the towers of Lisbon, but the Portuguese themselves were distrustful of our support, and the English troops, while daily preparing for embarcation, were compelled to assume a defensive attitude against those whose cause they were maintaining. But such was the prestige already attached to Wellesley's name that his arrival in the Tagus changed every feature of the scene. No longer suspicious of our intentions, the Portuguese Government gave prompt effect to the suggestions of the English commander; levies were decreed and organized, provisions collected, depôts established, and a spirit of confidence again pervaded the country, which was unqualified on this occa

4*

sion by that jealous distrust which had formerly neutralized its effects. The command in chief of the native army was intrusted to an English officer of great distinction, General Beresford, and no time was lost in once more testing the efficacy of the British arms.

Our description of the positions relatively occupied by the contending parties at this juncture will, perhaps, be remembered. Soult, having left Ney to control the north, was at Oporto, with 24,000 men, preparing to cross the Douro and descend upon Lisbon, while Victor and Lapisse, with 30,000 more, were to co-operate in the attack from the contiguous provinces of Estremadura and Leon. Of the Spanish armies we need only say that they had been repeatedly routed with more or less disgrace, though Cuesta still held a certain force together in the valley of the Tagus. There were therefore two courses open to the British commander—either to repel the menaced advance of Soult by marching on Oporto or to effect a junction with Cuesta, and try the result of a demonstration upon Madrid. The latter of these plans was wisely postponed for the moment, and, preference having been decisively given to the former, the troops at once commeneed their march upon the Douro. The British force under Sir Arthur Wellesley's command amounted at this time to about 20,000 men, to which about 15,000 Portuguese in a respectable state of organization were added by the exertions of Beresford. Of these about 24,000 were now led against Soult, who, though not inferior in strength, no sooner ascertained the advance of the English commander than he arranged for a retreat, by detaching Loison with 6,000 men to dislodge a Portuguese post in his left rear. Sir Arthur's intention was to envelope, if possible, the French corps by pushing forward a strong force upon its left, and then intercepting its retreat towards Ney's position, while the main body assaulted Soult in his quarters at Oporto. The former of these operations he intrusted to Beresford, the latter he directed in person. On the 12th of May the troops reached the southern bank of the Douro; the waters of which, 300 yards in width, rolled between them and their adversaries. In anticipation of the attack Soult had destroyed the floating-bridge, had collected all the boats on the opposite side, and there, with his forces well in hand for action or retreat, was looking from the window of his lodging, enjoying the presumed discomfiture of his opponent. To attempt such a passage as this in face of one of the ablest marshals of France was, indeed, an audacious stroke, but it was not beyond the daring of that genius which M. Thiers describes as calculated only for the stolid operations of defensive war. Availing himself of a point where the river by a bend in its course was not easily visible from the town, Sir Arthur determined on transporting, if possible, a few troops to the northern bank, and occupying an unfinished stone building, which he perceived was capable of affording temporary cover. The means were soon supplied by the activity of Colonel Waters—an officer whose habitual audacity rendered him one of the heroes of this memorable war. Crossing in a skiff to the opposite bank, he returned with two or three boats, and in a few minutes a company of the Buffs was established in the building. Reinforcements quickly followed, but not without discovery. The alarm was given, and presently the edifice was enveloped by the eager battalions of the French. The British, however, held their ground; a passage was effected at other points during the struggle; the French, after an ineffectual resistance, were fain to abandon the city in precipitation, and Sir Arthur, after his unexampled feat of arms, sat down that evening to the dinner which had been prepared for Soult. Nor did the disasters of the French marshal terminate here, for, though the designs of the British commander had been partially frustrated by the intelligence gained by the enemy, yet the French communications were so far intercepted, that Soult only joined Ney after losses and privations little short of those which had been experienced by Sir John Moore.

This brilliant operation being effected, Sir Arthur was now at liberty to turn to the main project of the campaign—that to which, in fact, the attack upon Soult had been subsidiary—the defeat of Victor in Estremadura; and, as the force under this marshal's command was not greater than that which had been so decisively defeated at Oporto, some confidence might naturally be entertained in calculating upon the result. But, at this time, the various difficulties of the English commander began to disclose themselves. Though his losses had been extremely small in the recent actions, considering the importance of their results, the troops were suffering severely from sickness, at least 4,000 being in hospital, while supplies of all kinds were miserably deficient, through the imperfections of the commissariat. The soldiers were nearly barefooted, their pay was largely in arrear, and the military chest was empty. In addition to this, although the real weakness of the Spanish armies was not yet fully known, it was clearly discernible that the character of their commanders would preclude any effective concert in the joint operations of the allied force. Cuesta would take no advice, and insisted on the adoption of his own schemes, with such obstinacy, that Sir Arthur was compelled to frame his plans accordingly. Instead, therefore, of circumventing Victor, as he had intended, he advanced into Spain at the beginning of July, to effect a junction with Cuesta, and feel his way towards Madrid. The armies, when united, formed a mass of 78,000 combatants; but, of these, 56,000 were Spanish, and for the brunt of war Sir Arthur could only reckon on his 22,000 British troops —Beresford's Portuguese having been despatched to the north of Portugal. On the other side, Victor's force had been strengthened by the succours which Joseph Bonaparte, alarmed for the safety of Madrid, had hastily concentrated at Toledo; and when the two armies at length confronted each other at Talavera, it was found that 55,000 excellent French troops were arrayed against Sir Arthur and his ally, while nearly as many more were descending from the north on the line of the British communications along the valley of the Tagus. On the 28th of July, the British Commander, after making the best dispositions in his power, received the attack of the French, directed by Joseph Bonaparte in person, with Victor and Jourdan at his side, and after an engagement of great severity, in which the Spaniards were virtually inactive, he remained master of the field against double his numbers, having repulsed the enemy at all points, with heavy loss, and having captured several hundred prisoners and seventeen pieces of cannon, in this, the first great pitched battle between the French and English in the Peninsula.

In this well fought field of Talavera, the French had thrown, for the first time, their whole disposable force upon the British army, without success; and Sir Arthur Wellesley inferred, with a justifiable confidence, that the relative superiority of his troops to those of the Emperor, was practically decided. Jomini, the French military historian, confesses almost as much, and the opinions of Napoleon himself, as visible in his correspondence, underwent from that moment a serious change. Yet at home, the people, wholly unaccustomed to the contingencies of a real war, and the Opposition, unscrupulously employing the delusions of the people, combined in decrying the victory, denouncing the successful general, and despairing of the whole enterprise. The city of London, even, recorded on a petition, its discontent with the "*rashness, ostentation, and useless valour*," of that commander whom M. Thiers depicts as endowed solely with the sluggish and phlegmatic tenacity of his countrymen; and though Ministers succeeded in procuring an acknowledgment of the services performed, and a warrant for persisting in the effort, both they and the British General were sadly cramped in the means of action. Sir Arthur Wellesley became, indeed, "Baron Douro, of Wellesley, and Viscount Wellington of Talavera, and of Wellington, in the county of Somerset;" but the Government was afraid to maintain his effective means even at the moderate amount for which he had stipulated, and they gave him plainly to understand that the responsibility of the war must rest upon his own shoulders. He accepted it, and, in full reliance on his own resources and the tried valour of his troops, awaited the shock which was at hand.

The battle of Talavera acted on the Emperor Napoleon exactly like the battle of Vimiera. His best soldiers had failed against those led by the "Sepoy General," and he became seriously alarmed for his conquest of Spain. After Vimiera he rushed, at the head of his guards, through Somosierra to Madrid; and now, after Talavera, he prepared a still more redoubtable invasion. Relieved from his continental liabilities by the campaigns of Aspern and Wagram, and from nearer apprehensions by the discomfiture of our expedition to Walcheren, he poured his now disposable legions in extraordinary numbers through the passes of the Pyrenees. Nine powerful corps, mustering fully 280,000 effective men, under Marshals Victor, Ney, Soult, Mortier, and Massena, with a crowd of aspiring generals besides, represented the force definitely charged with the final subjugation of the Peninsula. To meet the shock of this stupendous array Wellington had the 20,000 troops of Talavera augmented, besides other reinforcements, by that memorable brigade which, under the name of the Light Division, became afterwards the admiration of both armies. In addition, he had Beresford's Portuguese levies, now 30,000 strong, well disciplined, and capable, as events showed, of becoming first-rate soldiers, making a total of some 55,000 disposable troops, independent of garrisons and detachments. All hopes of effectual co-operation from Spain had now vanished. Disregarding the sage advice of Wellington, the Spanish generals had consigned themselves and their armies to inevitable destruction, and of the whole kingdom Gibraltar and Cadiz alone had escaped the swoop of the victorious French. The Provisional Administration displayed neither resolution nor sincerity, the British forces were suffered absolutely to starve, and Wellington was unable to extort from the leaders around him the smallest assistance for that army which was the last support of Spanish freedom. It was under such circumstances, with forces full of spirit, but numerically weak, without any assurance of sympathy at home, without money or supplies on the spot, and in the face of Napoleon's best marshal, with 80,000 troops in line, and 40,000 in reserve, that Wellington entered on the campaign of 1810—a campaign pronounced by military critics to be inferior to none in his whole career.

Withdrawing, after the victory of Talavera, from the concentrating forces of the enemy attracted by his advance, he had at first taken post on the Guadiana, until, wearied out by Spanish insincerity and perverseness, he moved his army to the Mondego, preparatory to those encounters which he foresaw the defence of Portugal must presently bring to pass. Already had he divined by his own sagacity the character and necessities of the coming campaign. Massena, as the best representative of the Emperor himself, having under his orders Ney, Regnier, and Junot, was gathering his forces on the north-eastern frontier of Portugal to fulfil his master's commands by "sweeping the English leopard into the sea." Against such hosts as he brought to the assault a defensive attitude was all that could be maintained, and Wellington's eye had detected the true mode of operation. He proposed to make the immediate district of Lisbon perform that service for Portugal which Portugal itself performed for the Peninsula at large, by furnishing an impregnable fastness and a secure retreat. By carrying lines of fortification from the Atlantic coast, through Torres Vedras, to the bank of the Tagus a little above Lisbon, he succeeded in constructing an artificial stronghold within which his retiring forces would be inaccessible, and from which, as opportunities invited, he might issue at will. These provisions silently and unobtrusively made, he calmly took post on the Coa, and awaited the assault. Hesitating or undecided, from some motive or other, Massena for weeks delayed the blow, till at length, after feeling the mettle of the Light Division on the Coa, he put his army in motion after the British commander, who slowly retired to his defences. Deeming, however, that a passage of arms would tend both to inspirit his own troops in what seemed like a retreat, and to teach Massena the true quality of the antagonist before him, he deliberately halted at Busaco and offered battle. Unable to refuse the challenge, the French marshal directed his bravest troops against the British position, but they were foiled with immense loss at every point of the attack, and Wellington proved, by one of his most brilliant victories, that his retreat partook neither of discomfiture nor fear. Rapidly recovering himself, however, Massena followed on his formidable foe, and was dreaming of little less than a second evacuation of Portugal, when, to his astonishment and dismay, he found himself abruptly arrested in his course by the tremendous lines of Torres Vedras.

These prodigious intrenchments comprised a triple line of fortifications one within the other, the innermost being intended to cover the embarcation of the troops in the last resort. The main strength of the works had been thrown on the second line, at which it had been intended to make the final stand, but even the outer barrier was found in effect to be so formidable as to deter the enemy from all hopes of a successful assault. Thus checked in mid career, the French marshal chafed and fumed in front of these impregnable lines, afraid to attack, yet unwilling to retire. For a whole month did he lie here inactive, tenacious of his purpose, though aware of his defeat, and eagerly watching for the first advantage which the chances of war or the mistakes of the British general might offer him. Meantime, however, while Wellington's concentrated forces were enjoying, through his sage provisions, the utmost comfort and abundance within their lines, the French army was gradually reduced to the last extremities of destitution and disease, and Massena at length broke up in despair, to commence a retreat which was never afterwards exchanged for an advance. Confident in hope and spirit, and overjoyed to see retiring before them one of those real Imperial armies which had swept the continent from the Rhine to the Vistula, the British troops issued from their works in hot pursuit, and, though the extraordinary genius of the French commander preserved his forces from what in ordinary cases would have been the ruin of a rout, yet his sufferings were so extreme and his losses so heavy that he carried to the frontier scarcely one-half of the force with which he had plunged blindly into Portugal. Following up his wary enemy with a caution which no success was permitted to disturb, Wellington presently availed himself of his position to attempt the recovery of Almeida, a fortress which, with Ciudad Rodrigo, forms the key of northeastern Portugal, and which had been taken by Massena in his advance. Anxious to preserve this important place, the French marshal turned with his whole force upon the foe, but Wellington met him at Fuentes d'Onoro, repulsed his attempts in a sanguinary engagement, and Almeida fell.

As at this point the tide of French conquest had been actually turned, and the British army, so lightly held by Napoleon, was now manifestly chasing his eagles from the field, it might have been presumed that popularity and support would have rewarded the unexampled successes of the English general. Yet it was not so. The reverses experienced during the same period in Spain were loudly appealed to as neutralizing the triumphs in Portugal, and at no moment was there a more vehement denunciation of the whole Peninsular war. Though Cadiz resolutely held out, and Graham, indeed, on the heights of Barossa, had emulated the glories of Busaco, yet even the strong fortress of Badajoz had now fallen before the vigorous audacity of Soult; and Suchet, a rising general of extraordinary abilities, was effecting by the reduction of hitherto impregnable strongholds the complete conquest of Catalonia and Valencia. Eagerly turning these disasters to account, and inspirited by the accession of the Prince Regent to power, the Opposition in the British Parliament so oppressed the Ministry, that at the very moment when Wellington, after his unrivalled strategy, was on the track of his retreating foe, he could scarcely count for common support on the Government he was serving. He was represented in England, as his letters show us, to be "in a scrape," and he fought with the consciousness that all his reverses would be magnified and all his successes denied. Yet he failed neither in heart nor hand. He had verified all his own assertions respecting the defensibility of Portugal. His army had become a perfect model in discipline and daring, he was driving before him 80,000 of the best troops of the Empire, and he relied on the resources of his own genius for compensating those disadvantages to which he foresaw he must be still exposed. Such was the campaign of 1810,—better conceived and worse appreciated than any which we shall have to record.

As the maintenance of Portugal was subsidiary to the great object of the war,—the deliverance of the Peninsula from French domination,—Wellington of course proceeded, after successfully repulsing the invaders from Portuguese soil, to assume the offensive, by carrying his arms into Spain. Thus, after defeating Junot, he had been induced to try the battle of Talavera; and now, after expelling Massena, he betook himself to similar designs, with this difference—that instead of operating by the valley of the Tagus against Madrid, he now moved to the valley of the Guadiana for the purpose of recovering Badajoz, a fortress, like that of Ciudad Rodrigo, so critically situated on the frontier, that with these two places in the enemy's hands, as they now were, it became hazardous either to quit Portugal or to penetrate into Spain. At this point, therefore, were now to commence the famous sieges of the

Peninsula—sieges which will always reflect immortal honor on the troops engaged, and which will always attract the interest of the English reader; but which must, nevertheless, be appealed to as illustrations of the straits to which an army may be led by want of military experience in the Government at home. By this time the repeated victories of Wellington and his colleagues had raised the renown of British soldiers to at least an equality with that of Napoleon's veterans, and the incomparable efficiency, in particular, of the light division was acknowledged to be without a parallel in any European service. But in those departments of the army where excellence is less the result of intuitive ability, the forces under Wellington were still greatly surpassed by the trained legions of the Emperor. While Napoleon had devoted his whole genius to the organization of the parks and trains which attend the march of an army in the field, the British troops had only the most imperfect resources on which to rely. The Engineer corps, though admirable in quality, was so deficient in numbers that commissions were placed at the free disposal of Cambridge mathematicians. The siege trains were weak and worthless against the solid ramparts of Peninsula strongholds, the intrenching tools were so ill made that they snapped in the hands of the workmen, and the art of sapping and mining was so little known that this branch of the siege duties was carried on by draughts from regiments of the line, imperfectly and hastily instructed for the purpose. Unhappily, these results can only be obviated by long foresight, patient training, and costly provision; it was not in the power of a single mind, however capacious, to effect an instantaneous reform, and Wellington was compelled to supply the deficiencies by the best blood of his troops.

The command of the force commissioned to recover Badajoz had been intrusted to Marshal Beresford until Lord Wellington could repair in person to the scene, and it was against Soult, who was marching rapidly from the South to the relief of the place, that the glorious but sanguinary battle of ALBUERA was fought on the 16th of May. Having checked the enemy by this bloody defeat Beresford resumed his duties of the siege until he was superseded by the Commander-in-Chief. But all the efforts of Wellington and his troops were vain, for the present, against this celebrated fortress; two assaults were repulsed, and the British general determined on relinquishing the attempt, and returning to the northern frontier of Portugal for more favourable opportunities of action. He had now by his extraordinary genius so far changed the character of the war, that the British, heretofore fighting with desperate tenacity for a footing at Lisbon or Cadiz, were now openly assuming the offensive, and Napoleon had been actually compelled to direct defensive preparations along the road leading through Vittoria to Bayonne—that very road which Wellington in spite of these defences was soon to traverse in triumph. Meantime fresh troops were pouring over the Pyrenees into Spain, and a new plan of operations was dictated by the Emperor himself. One powerful army in the north was to guard Castile and Leon, and watch the road by which Wellington might be expected to advance; another, under Soult, strongly reinforced, was to maintain French interests in

Andalusia and menace Portugal from the south; while Marmont, who had succeeded Massena, took post with 30,000 men in the valley of the Tagus, resting on Toledo and Madrid, and prepared to concert movements with either of his colleagues as occasion might arise. To encounter these antagonists, who could rapidly concentrate 90,000 splendid troops against him, Wellington could barely bring 50,000 into the field; and though this disparity of numbers was afterwards somewhat lessened, yet it is scarcely in reason to expect that even the genius of Wellington or the valour of his troops could have ultimately prevailed against such odds but for circumstances which favoured the designs of the British and rendered the contest less unequal. In the first place, the jealousies of the French marshals, when unrepressed by the Emperor's presence, were so inveterate as to disconcert the best operations, being sometimes little less suicidal than those of the Princes of India. Next, although the Spanish armies had ceased to offer regular resistance to the invaders, yet the guerilla system of warfare, aided by interminable insurrections, acted to the incessant embarrassment of the French, whose duties, perils, and fatigues were doubled by the restless activity of these daring enemies. But the most important of Wellington's advantages was that of position. With an impregnable retreat at Lisbon, with free water carriage in his rear, and with the great arteries of the Douro and the Tagus for conducting his supplies, he could operate at will from his central fastness towards the north, east, or south. If the northern provinces were temporarily disengaged from the enemy's presence, he could issue by Almeida and Salamanca upon the great line of communication between the Pyrenees and Madrid; if the valley of the Tagus were left unguarded, he could march directly upon the capital by the well-known route of Talavera; while if Soult, by any of these demonstrations, was tempted to cross the Guadiana, he could carry his arms into Andalusia by Elvas and Badajoz. Relying, too, on the excellence of his troops, he confidently accounted himself a match for any single army of the enemy, while he was well aware, from the exhausted state of the country and the difficulties of procuring subsistence no concentration of the French forces could be maintained for many days together. In this way, availing himself of the far superior intelligence which he enjoyed through the agency of the guerillas, and of his own exclusive facilities for commanding supplies, he succeeded in paralysing the enormous hosts of Napoleon, by constant alarms and well-directed blows, till at length when the time of action came he advanced from cantonments and drove King Joseph and all his marshals headlong across the Pyrenees.

The position taken up by Wellington when he transferred his operations from the south to the north frontier of Portugal was at Fuente Guinaldo, a locality possessing some advantageous features in the neigbourhood of Ciudad Rodrigo. His thoughts being still occupied by the means of gaining the border fortresses, he had promptly turned to Rodrigo from Badajoz, and had arranged his plans with a double prospect of success. Knowing that the place was inadequately provisioned he conceived hopes of blockading it into submission from his post at Fuente Guinaldo, since in the presence of this force no supplies could be thrown into the town unless escorted by a convoy equal to the army under his command. Either, therefore, the French marshal must abandon Rodrigo to its fate, or he must go through the difficult operation of concentrating all his forces to form the convoy required. Marmont chose the latter alternative, and uniting his army with that of Dorsenne advanced to the relief of Rodrigo with an immense train of stores and 60,000 fighting men. By this extraordinary effort not only was the place provisioned, but Wellington himself was brought into a situation of some peril, for after successfully repulsing an attempt of the French in the memorable combat of El Bodon he found himself the next day, with only 15,000 men actually at his disposal, exposed to the attack of the entire French army. Fortunately Marmont was unaware of the chance thus offered him, and while he was occupying himself in evolutions and displays, Wellington collected his troops and stood once more in security on his position. This movement, however, of the French commander destroyed all hopes of reducing Rodrigo by blockade, and the British general recurred accordingly to the alternative he had been contemplating of an assault by force.

To comprehend the difficulties of this enterprise, it must be remembered that the superiority of strength was indisputably with the French whenever they concentrated their forces, and that it was certain such concentration would be attempted, at any risk, to save such a place as Rodrigo. Wellington, therefore, had to prepare, with such secrecy as to elude the suspicions of his enemy, the enormous mass of materials required for such a siege as that he projected. As the town stood on the opposite or Spanish bank of the river Agueda, and as the approaches were commanded by the guns of the garrison, it became necessary to construct a temporary bridge. Moreover, the heavy battering train, which alone required 5000 bullocks to draw it, had to be brought up secretly to the spot, though it was a work almost of impossibility to get a score of cattle together. But these difficulties were surmounted by the inventive genius of the British commander. Preparing his battering train at Lisbon, he shipped it at that port as if for Cadiz, transhipped it into smaller craft at sea, and then brought it up the stream of the Douro. In the next place, he succeeded, beyond the hopes of his engineers, in rendering the Douro navigable for a space of 40 miles beyond the limit previously presumed, and at length he collected the whole necessary materials in the rear of his army without any knowledge on the part of his antagonist. He was now to reap the reward of his precaution and skill. Towards the close of the year the French armies having—conformably to directions of the Emperor, framed entirely on the supposition that Wellington had no heavy artillery—been dispersed in cantonments, the Bristish general suddenly threw his bridge across the Agueda, and besieged CIUDAD RODRIGO in force. Ten days only elapsed between the investment and the storm. On the 8th of January, 1812, the Agueda was crossed, and on the 19th the British were in the city. The loss of life greatly exceeded the limit assigned to such expenditure in the scientific calculations of military engineers; but the enterprise was undertaken in the face of a superior force, which could at once have defeated it by appearing on the scene of action; and so effectually was Marmont baffled by the vigour of the British that the place had fallen before his army was collected for its relief. The repetition of such a stroke at Badajoz, which was now Wellington's aim, presented still greater difficulties, for the vigilance of the French was alarmed, the garrison of the place had been reconstituted by equal draughts from the various armies in order to interest each marshal personally in its relief, and Soult in Andalusia, like Marmont in Castile, possessed a force competent to overwhelm any covering army which Wellington could detach. Yet on the 7th of April BADAJOZ likewise fell, and after opening a new campaign with these famous demonstrations of his own sagacity and the courage of his troops, he prepared for a third time to advance definitely from Portugal into Spain.

Though the forces of Napoleon in the Peninsula were presently to be somewhat weakened by the requirements of the Russian war, yet at the moment when these strongholds were wrenched from their grasp the ascendency of the Emperor was yet uncontested, and from the Niemen to the Atlantic there was literally no resistance to his universal dominion save by this army, which was clinging with invincible tenacity to the rocks of Portugal, at the western extremity of Europe. From these well defended lines, however, they were now to emerge, and while Hill, by his surprise of Gerard at ARROYO MOLINOS and his brilliant capture of the forts at the bridge of ALMARAZ, was alarming the French for the safety of Andalusia, Wellington began his march to the Pyrenees. On this occasion he was at first unimpeded. So established was the reputation of the troops and their general that Marmont retired as he advanced, and Salamanca, after four years of oppressive occupation, was evacuated before the liberating army. But the hosts into which Wellington had thus boldly plunged with 40,000 troops still numbered fully 270,000 soldiers, and though these forces were divided by distance and jealousies, Marmont had no difficulty in collecting an army numerically superior to that of his antagonist. Returning, therefore, to the contest, and hovering about the English general for the opportunity of pouncing at an advantage upon his troops, he gave promise of a decisive battle, and, after some days of elaborate manœuvring, the opposing armies found themselves confronted, on the 22d of July, in the vicinity of SALAMANCA. It was a trial of strategy, but in strategy as well as vigour the French marshal was surpassed by his redoubtable adversary. Seizing with intuitive genius an occasion which Marmont offered, Wellington fell upon his army and routed it so completely that half of its effective force was destroyed in the engagement. So decisively had the blow been dealt, and so skilfully had it been directed, that, as Napoleon had long foretold of such an event, it paralysed the entire French force in Spain, and reduced it to the relative position so long maintained by the English—that of tenacious defence. The only two considerable armies now remaining were those of Suchet in the east, and Soult in the south. Suchet, on hearing of Marmont's defeat, proposed that the French should make a Portugal of their own in Catalonia, and defend themselves in its fastnesses till aid could arrive from the Pyrenees;

while Soult advocated with equal warmth a retirement into Andalusia and a concentration behind the Guadiana. There was little time for deliberation, for Wellington was hot upon his prey, but as King Joseph decamped from his capital he sent orders to Soult to evacuate Andalusia; and the victorious army of the British, after thus, by a single blow, clearing half Spain of its invaders, made its triumphant entry into Madrid.

Wellington was now in possession of the capital of Spain. He had succeeded in delivering that blow which had so long been meditated, and had signalized the growing ascendency of his army by the total defeat of his chief opponent in open field. But his work was far from finished, and while all around was rejoicing and triumph, his forecast was anxiously revolving the imminent contingencies of the war. In one sense, indeed, the recent victory had increased rather than lessened the dangers of his position, for it had driven his adversaries by force of common peril into a temporary concert, and Wellington well knew that any such concert would reduce him again to the defensive. Marshal Soult, it was true, had evacuated Andalusia, and King Joseph Madrid; but their forces had been carried to Suchet's quarters in Valencia, where they would thus form an overpowering concentration of strength; and in like manner, though Marmont's army had been shorn of half its numbers, it was rapidly recovering itself under Clauzel by the absorption of all the detachments which had been operating in the north. Wellington saw, therefore, that he must prepare himself for a still more decisive struggle, if not for another retreat;

and conceiving it most important to disembarrass his rear, he turned round upon Clauzel with the intention of crushing him before he could be fully reinforced, and thus establishing himself securely on the line of the Douro to await the advance of King Joseph from the east.

With these views, after leaving a strong garrison at Madrid, he put his army in motion, drove Clauzel before him from Valladolid, and on the 18th of September appeared before BURGOS. This place, though not a fortification of the first rank, had been recently strengthened by the orders of Napoleon, whose sagacity had divined the use to which its defences might possibly be turned. It lay in the great road to Bayonne, and was now one of the chief depôts retained by the French in the Peninsula, for the campaign had stripped them of Rodrigo, Badajoz, Madrid, Salamanca, and Seville. It became, therefore, of great importance to effect its reduction, and Wellington sat down before it with a force which, although theoretically unequal to the work, might, perhaps, from past recollections, have warranted some expectations of success. But our Peninsular sieges supply, as we have said, rather warnings than examples. Badajoz and Rodrigo were only won by a profuse expenditure of life, and Burgos, though attacked with equal intrepidity, was not won at all. After consuming no less than five weeks before its walls Wellington gave reluctant orders for raising the siege and retiring. It was, indeed, time, for the Northern army, now under the command of Souham, mustered 44,000 men in his rear, and Soult and Joseph were advancing with fully 70,000 more upon the Tagus. To oppose these forces Wellington had only 33,000 troops, Spaniards included, under his immediate command, while Hill, with the garrison of Madrid, could only muster some 20,000 to resist the advances of Soult. The British commander determined, therefore, on recalling Hill from Madrid and resuming his former position on the Agueda—a resolution which he successfully executed in the face of the difficulties around him, though the suffering and discouragement of the troops during this unwelcome retreat were extremely severe. A detailed criticism of these operations would be beyond our province. It is enough to say that the French made a successful defence, and we have no occasion to begrudge them the single achievement against the English arms which could be contributed to the historic gallery of Versailles by the whole Peninsular War.

Such, however, was in those times the incredulity or perverseness of party spirit in England that, while no successes were rated at their true import, every incomplete operation was magnified into a disaster, and described as a warning. The retreat from Burgos was cited, like the retreat from Talavera, as a proof of the mismanagement of the war; and occasion was taken in Parliament to compare even the victory of Salamanca with the battles of Marlborough, to the disparagement of Wellington and his army. Nor did any great enlightenment yet prevail on the subject of military operations; for a considerable force, destined to act on the eastern coast of Spain, was diverted by Lord William Bentinck to Sicily at a moment when its appearance in Valencia would have disconcerted all the plans of the French, and, by providing occupation for Joseph and his marshals, have relieved Wellington from that concentration of his enemies before which he was compelled to retire. But neither the wilfulness of faction nor the tenacity of folly could do more than obstruct events which were now steadily in course. Even the inherent obstinacy of Spanish character had at length yielded to the visible genius of Wellington, and the whole military force of the country was now at length, in the fifth year of the war, placed under his paramount command. But these powers were little more than nominal; and, in order to derive an effective support from the favourable disposition of the Spanish Government, the British general availed himself of the winter season to repair in person to Cadiz.

It will be remembered that when, after the battle of Talavera and the retirement of Wellington to Portugal, the French poured their accumulated legions into Andalusia, Cadiz alone had been preserved from the deluge. Since that time the troops of Soult had environed it in vain. Secured by a British garrison, strongly fortified by nature, and well supplied from the sea, it was in little danger of capture; and it discharged, indeed, a substantial service, by detaining a large detachment from the general operations of the war. In fact, the French could scarcely be described as besieging it; for, though they maintained their guard with unceasing vigilance, it was at so respectful a distance, that the great mortar which now stands in St. James's Park was cast especially for this extraordinary length of range; and their own position was entrenched with an anxiety sufficiently indicative of their anticipations. Exempted in this manner from many of the troubles of war while cooped in the narrow space of a single town, the Spanish patriots enjoyed ample liberty of political discussion, and the fermentation of spirits was proportionate to the occasion. It was here that the affairs of the war, as regarded the Spanish armies, were regulated by a popular assembly under the control of a licentious mob; and it was here that those democratic principles of government were first promulgated which in later times so intimately affected the fortunes of the Peninsular monarchies. "The Cortes," wrote Wellington, "have framed a Constitution very much on the principle that a painter paints a picture—viz., to be looked at. I have not met any person of any description who considers that Spain either is or can be governed by such a system." From this body, however, the British commander succeeded in temporarily obtaining the power he desired, and he returned to Portugal prepared to open, with invigorated spirit and confidence, the campaign of 1813.

Several circumstances now combined to promise a decisive turn in the operations of the war. The initiative, once taken by Wellington, had been never lost, and although he had retrograded from Burgos, it was without any discomfiture at the hands of the enemy. The reinforcements despatched from England, though proportioned neither to the needs of the war nor the resources of the country, were considerable, and the effective strength of the army—a term which excludes the Spanish contingents—reached to full 70,000 men. On the other hand, the reverses of Napoleon in the

Russian campaign had not only reduced his forces in the Peninsula, but had rendered it improbable that they could be succoured on any emergency with the same promptitude as before. Above all, Wellington himself was now unfettered in his command; for if the direction in chief of the Spanish armies brought but little direct accession of strength, it at any rate relieved him from the necessity of concerting operations with generals on whose discretion he had found it impossible to rely. These considerations, coupled with an instinctive confidence in his dispositions for the campaign, and an irresistible presage of the success which at length awaited his patience, so inspired the British commander that, in putting his troops once more in motion for Spain, he rose in his stirrups as the frontier was passed, and waving his hat, exclaimed prophetically, "Farewell, Portugal!" Events soon verified the finality of this adieu, for a few short months carried the "Sepoy General" in triumph to Paris.

At the commencement of the famous campaign of 1813, the material superiority still lay apparently with the French, for King Joseph disposed of a force little short of 200,000 men—a strength exceeding that of the army under Wellington's command—even if all denominations of troops are included in the calculation. But the British general reasonably concluded that he had by this time experienced the worst of what the enemy could do. He knew that the difficulties of subsistence, no less than the jealousies of the several commanders, would render any large or permanent concentration impossible, and he had satisfactorily measured the power of his own army against any likely to be brought into the field against him. He confidently calculated, therefore, on making an end of the war; his troops were in the highest spirits, and the lessons of the retreat from Burgos had been turned to seasonable advantage. In comparison with his previous restrictions all might now be said to be in his own hands, and the result of the change was soon made conclusively manifest.

Hitherto, as we have seen, the offensive movements of Wellington from his Portuguese stronghold had been usually directed against Madrid, by one of the two great roads of Salamanca or Talavera, and the French had been studiously led to anticipate similar dispositions on the present occasion. Under such impressions they collected their main strength on the north bank of the Douro, to defend that river to the last, intending, as Wellington moved upon Salamanca, to fall on his left flank by the bridges of Toro and Zamora. The British general, however, had conceived a very different plan of operations. Availing himself of preparations carefully made, and information anxiously collected, he moved the left wing of his army through a province hitherto untraversed to the north bank of the Douro, and then, after demonstrations at Salamanca, suddenly joining it with the remainder of the army, he took the French defences in reverse, and showed himself in irresistible force on the line of their communications. The effect was decisive. Constantly menaced by the British left, which was kept steadily in advance, Joseph evacuated one position after another without hazarding an engagement, blew up the castle of Burgos in the precipitancy of his retreat, and only took post at VITTORIA to experience the most conclusive defeat ever sustained by the French arms since the battle of Blenheim. His entire army was routed, with inconsiderable slaughter, but with irrecoverable discomfiture. All the plunder of the Peninsula fell into the hands of the victors. Jourdan's *bâton*, and Joseph's travelling carriage became the trophies of the British general, and the walls of Apsley-house display to this hour in their most precious ornaments the spoils of this memorable battle. The occasion was improved as skilfully as it had been created. Pressing on his retiring foe, Wellington drove him into the recesses of the Pyrenees, and surrounding the frontier fortresses of St. Sebastian and Pampeluna, prepared to maintain the mountain passes against a renewed invasion. His anticipations of the future proved correct. Detaching what force he could spare from his own emergencies, Napoleon sent Soult again with plenary powers to retrieve the credit and fortunes of the army. Impressed with the peril of the crisis, and not disguising the abilities of the commander opposed to him, this able "Lieutenant of the Emperor" collected his whole strength, and suddenly poured with impetuous valor through the passes of the PYRENEES, on the isolated posts of his antagonist. But at MAYA and SORAUVEN the French were once more repulsed by the vigorous determination of the British; ST. SEBASTIAN, after a sanguinary siege, was carried by storm, and on the 9th of November, four months after the battle of Vittoria, Wellington slept, for the last time during the war, on the territory of the Peninsula. The BIDASSOA and the NIVELLE were successfully crossed in despite of all the resistance which Soult could oppose, and the British army, which five years before, amid the menacing hosts of the enemy and the ill-boding omens of its friends, had maintained a precarious footing on the crags of Portugal, now bivouacked in uncontested triumph on the soil of France. With these strokes the mighty game had at length been won, for though Soult clung with convulsive tenacity to every defensible point of ground, and though at TOULOUSE he drew such vigour from despair as suggested an equivocal claim to the honours of the combat, yet the result of the struggle was now beyond the reach of fortune. Not only was Wellington advancing in irresistible strength, but Napoleon himself had succumbed to his more immediate antagonists; and the French marshals, discovering themselves without authority or support, desisted from hostilities which had become both gratuitous and hopeless.

Thus terminated, with unexampled glory to England and its army, the great Peninsular War—a struggle commenced with ambiguous views and prosecuted with doubtful expectations, but carried to a triumphant conclusion by the extraordinary genius of a single man. We are not imputing any prodigies of heroism to the conquerors or their chief. None knew better than he who is now gone that war was no matter of romance, but a process obeying in its course the self-same rules which humanly determine the success of all national undertakings. It is undoubtedly true, as we have been describing, that Wellington, with a heterogeneous force rarely exceeding 50,000 effective troops, and frequently far below even this disproportionate amount, did first repel, then attack, and ultimately vanquish, a host of foes comprising from 200,000 to 350,000 of the finest soldiers of the French Empire, led by its most renowned commanders; and such a feat of arms does, indeed, appear to savour of the heroïc or supernatural. But the game was always in reality on the cards. The mighty armies of the French were not practically available for a concentrated effort. The jealousies of the several marshals, and the caprices of their nominal Sovereign, precluded any systematic co-operation between them, and the necessities of subsistence in a rude and hostile country effectually prevented the assemblage for any lengthened period of a larger force than the British commander had proved his ability to encounter. The campaigns of Talavera and Salamanca showed Wellington that his army was not likely, under proper precautions, to be overmatched in the field; experience soon taught him the limit of reinforcements from France. In the next place, the embarrassments and responsibilities of the French were greatly augmented by their own system of tactics and by the determined enmity of the Spaniards. Relying, according to Napoleon's principle, for the support of the war on the war itself, they were compelled to alienate the people of the country by ruthless plunder, and to make a fortified post of every depôt and magazine. As the guerilla practice gathered strength their communications were intercepted in every direction, and they commanded not an inch of territory beyond their immediate quarters. If they quitted a province, they lost it; if they evacuated a post for a moment, it was seized by enemies who were powerless against them in open field, but who hung with invincible hostility on their flanks and rear. On the other hand, Wellington commanded a compact army in a central position, from which he could operate in any direction at pleasure. Having conclusively proved, against even the tenacity and genius of Massena, that his own post was impregnable, he could strike at will to the right or the left; he could menace Soult in Andalusia, or Clauzel in Gallicia, or alarm King Joseph for his throne by marching upon Madrid. He was independent of the necessities which so crippled his antagonists. The sea was his own, and every port between Lisbon and Santander could be turned into a base of operations and an unfailing source of supplies. He knew that at the worst he could hold Portugal against all the might of France, and that there lay obedient to his baton an army competent to seize and improve every opportunity which time might bring—opportunities which could hardly be lacking under a system so hollow and unsubstantial as that on which Napoleon's power was reared. These are the conditions, explanatory in some degree of the result of the war; but they are in no wise disparaging to those extraordinary talents which conducted it to its conclusion. But for Wellington these chances would have been wholly unimproved and lost. It is his transcendent merit that he descried these promising circumstances when they were hidden from most and denied by all. He first detected the capabilities of Portugal as a defensive position; he first indicated the weak points of his antagonists; he first inspired confidence in his soldiers. To realize the favourable chances of the war, it was required that no act of imprudence should compromise the safety of that army on which all depended; that no means should be spared to maintain its efficiency and to create a subsidiary force in the levies of the country; that temptations should be resisted, obloquy disregarded, and provocations passed by. All this Wellington did, and did, too, not only without support, but in despite of discouragement. He never could persuade his countrymen of their real duties or prospects. They were extravagantly elated at his first success, and proportionately desponding afterwards. He could never teach them to look into the future or to believe in the value of a victory which fell short of a conquest. For a long time it may be said that he conducted the war on his own responsibility alone; for the Ministry, even when favourably disposed, were unable to send him adequate succours, and there was an Opposition ever ready to prophesy and denounce calamities which they were doing their best to occasion. On the spot, too, he was calumniated and thwarted in every possible way by the very people whose cause he was sustaining. The Spanish Generals encumbered his movements, while the Spanish Government, under the dictation of the populace of Cadiz, violated every engagement with him as soon as it was made. Yet, under all these circumstances, he persevered. He alone, at an early period, detected the essential unsoundness of the French power, and reiterated his assurances of eventual success. He argued with his own Government, temporized with his Spanish colleagues, and even convinced the patriot mob. By incessant exertions and extraordinary skill he raised a body of militiamen and recruits into an army unparalleled for its excellence, and by a succession of victories he at length taught his discontented countrymen to know their own military capacities and to believe in the fortune of their arms. It was this gradual creation of means and power which communicated so distinctive a character to the war. Sir Arthur Wellesley originally sailed with a handful of troops on an "expedition" to Portugal. He returned the commander of such a British army as had never before been seen, and the conqueror in such a war as had never before been maintained. Single-handed, England had encountered and defeated those redoubtable legions of France before which Continental Europe had hitherto succumbed. She had become a principal in the great European struggle, and, by the talents and fortune of her great commander, had entitled herself to no second place in the councils of the world. It is as well, perhaps, that our subject demands no special notice of that invincible army by which these feats were wrought. When the war was summarily concluded by the ruin of one of the belligerents, it had penetrated the French territory as far as Bordeaux. There it was broken up. Of its famous regiments, some were carried across the Atlantic to be launched heedlessly against the redoubts of New Orleans, some shipped off to perish in the rice swamps of Antigua, and some retained to participate in one more battle for victory. But from this point its renown lives in history alone; its merits never met the recognition which was their due, and our own generation has witnessed the tardy acknowledgment, by a piece of riband and a medal, of deeds which forty years before proved the salvation of Europe and the immortal glory of Britain.

During the memorable events which we have been describing, the character and position of Wellington had risen to a signal pitch of reputation and esteem. A successful soldier and a popular commander he had been accounted from the beginning, but he was now recognized as something infinitely more. By degrees the Spanish war had become a conspicuous element in the mighty European struggle; and it was the only war, indeed, in which an ascendant was permanently maintained over the star of Napoleon. All eyes were therefore turned upon the General enjoying such an exclusive privilege of genius or fortune. Nor were his merits limited to the field of battle alone. He was the visible adviser of Spanish and Portuguese statesmen, and whatever administrative successes awaited their efforts were due to no counsels but his. His clear vision and steady judgment disentangled all the intricacies of democratic intrigues or courtly corruption, and detected at once the path of wisdom and policy. It was impossible, too, that his views should be confined to the Peninsula. In those days all politics wore a cosmopolitan character. There was but one great question before the eyes of the world—European freedom or European servitude,—the "French Empire" on one side and a coalition of adversaries or victims on the other. Wellington's eye was cast over the plains of Germany, over the wilds of Russia, on the shores of the Baltic, and the islands of the Mediterranean. His sagacity estimated every combination at its true import, and measured the effects of every expedition, while his victories served to check despondency, or animate resistance in countries far removed from the scene of his operations. The battle of Salamanca was celebrated by the retiring Russians with rejoicings which fell ominously on the ears of their pursuers, and the triumph of Vittoria determined the wavering policy of Austria against the tottering fortunes of Napoleon. These circumstances lent a weight to the words of Wellington such as had rarely been before experienced either by statesman or soldier. On all points relating to the one great problem of the day, his opinion was anxiously asked and respectfully received—and not by his own Government alone, but by all Cabinets concerned in the prosecution of the pending struggle. When, therefore, the dissolution of Napoleon's empire compelled a new organization of France, the Duke of Wellington was promptly despatched to Paris, as the person most competent to advise and instruct the new Administration—four days only elapsing between his departure from the head of the army and his appearance as British Ambassador at the Tuileries. Within a week, again, of this time he was precipitately recalled to Madrid, as the only individual who, by his experience, knowledge, and influence, could compose the differences between the Spanish people and their malicious Sovereign; and before six months had passed, he was on his way to Vienna as the representative of his country in the great congress of nations which was to determine the settlement of the world. These practical testimonies to his renown throw wholly into the shade those incidental honours and decorations by which national acknowledgments are conveyed, and it is almost superfluous to add, that all the titles and distinctions at the command of Crowns and Cabinets were showered upon the liberator of the Peninsula and the conqueror of Napoleon. Talavera had made him a baron and a viscount; Ciudad Rodrigo an earl, Salamanca a marquis, and Vittoria a duke; and, as these honors had all accumulated in his absence, his successive patents were read together in a single day, as he took his seat for the first time, and with the highest rank, among the peers of England.

But his military services were not yet quite concluded—they were to terminate in a more brilliant though not more substantial triumph than had been won on the fields of Spain. While the allied Sovereigns were wrangling over the trophies of their success, their terrible antagonist re-appeared once more. Napoleon was again in Paris, and, aided by the devotion of his adherents, the military capacities of the nation, and the numbers of veteran soldiers who at the peace had been released from imprisonment, he speedily advanced at the head of an army as formidable as that of Austerlitz or Friedland. At the first rumours of war the contingent of England had been intrusted to Wellington, who occupied in Belgium the post of honour and peril. Of all the mighty reinforcements announced none but a Prussian corps was at hand, when, without warning given, the French Emperor fell headlong on his enemies at Ligny and Quatre Bras. The Duke had sketched out a scheme of hostilities with his usual decision, and was prepared to take the field with his usual confidence, but the loss of that army which "could go any where and do any thing" was now grievously felt. The troops of Napoleon were the very finest of the Empire—the true representatives of the Grand Army; but Wellington's motley force comprised only 33,000 British, and of these only a portion was contributed by the redoubtable old regiments of the Peninsula. Nevertheless, with these in the front line, and with Brunswickers, Belgians, Dutch and Germans in support, the British general awaited at Waterloo the impetuous onset of Napoleon, and at length won that crowning victory which is even yet familiar to the minds of Englishmen. That this final conquest added much more than brilliancy to the honours of Wellington is what cannot be said. The campaign was not long enough for strategy, nor was the battle fought by manœuvres; but whatever could be done by a general was done by England's Duke, and this distinct, and, as it were, personal conflict between the two great commanders of the age, naturally invested the conqueror with a peculiar lustre of renown.

By a destiny unexampled in history, the hero of these countless conquests survived to give more than one generation of his countrymen the benefit of his civil services. Such an ordeal has never before been endured by any public character. Military experience does not furnish the fittest schools of statesmanship, especially when the country to be governed is that of a free, intelligent, and progressive people. But, if the political principles of the great man who has now departed were not always reconcilable with the opinions and demands of modern advancement, they were at least consistent in themselves, were never extravagantly pressed, never tyrannically promoted, and never insisted on to the hindrance of the Government or the damage of the State. In estimating Wellington's politics it must never be forgotten that he was a politician of 1807, and that he descended to us the last representative of a school that had passed. If he was less liberally-minded than the statesmen of his later days, we may fairly inquire how many of his own generation would have been as liberal as he?

Our memoir now enters upon a period of history entirely new. The great battle of Waterloo had finally terminated the times of war, and introduced a reign of peace so stable, that its conclusion, notwithstanding some disturbances, may yet, we trust, be distant still. The condition of Europe which now ensued was exceedingly remarkable. The mighty contest just closed had been a struggle between two principles, which, though they assumed the forms of legitimacy and revolution, included also respectively the more moderate types of conservatism and reform. To all appearances the desperate game had been at length decided in favour of the party of resistance against the party of progress, and an undisputed sway might now have been anticipated for the ancient traditions of government. Yet the echoes of the cannon had scarcely ceased when the clamours of the people began, and political agitation was commenced with such advantage, popularity, and success as it had never enjoyed during the ascendency of revolutionary France. The explanation of this phenomenon is simple enough. The cessation of war and its vicissitudes had left a void in the popular mind. National spirits required new occupation, and the creation of some new interest to satisfy the desires which had been called into being by so exciting a struggle. But with this tendency to agitation in general was combined a decided bias in the direction of liberalism.

Much of the work of the French Revolutionists was imperishable, and many of their maxims survived the scaffolds of the Republic and the wars of the Empire. Topics, moreover, and novelties of all kinds had been tossed up by the political storm; discussion had been earnest, and Sovereigns, in the exigencies of a struggle for life and death, had been induced to concede something and promise more to the reasonable claims of their subjects. Moreover, the pressure of taxation was severely felt, and there was a natural desire to direct again to the proper objects of peace those energies of government which had been so long absorbed in the prosecution of war. The Duke of Wellington himself, in advocating certain measures of European policy at this period, observed with his unerring sagacity, that what was needed by the several Governments was such a peace as would give them "the power of reducing their overgrown military establishments, and the leisure to attend to the internal concerns of their nations, and to improve the situation of their people."

These conditions of society determined the character of European history during what has been termed "the 30 years' peace," and through which period we shall now have to follow the subject of our memoir. At the outset it appeared as if Sovereigns were not indisposed to share with the people that freedom to which the exertions of the latter had restored them, but, whether scared by visions of reviving Jacobinism or spoiled by the sweets of power, they speedily renounced their views, and concerted a common policy of repression throughout the whole of Europe. With the events which ensued we are no further concerned than in so far as they illustrate the position and conduct of the great Duke in mitigating or controlling them. In Germany and Italy the fires of discontent smouldered, with occasional outbreaks, until the conflagration of 1848. In France the process was so much more rapid that within 12 years of the evacuation of that country by the allied forces, the Duke lived to see flying on the Thames in harmony and concord with the flag of England that very tricolour which his whole military life had been devoted to debasing. What happened in England under this new system of politics we shall presently be called upon to relate.

The civil career of the Duke of Wellington thus divides itself into two portions, in one of which he cooperated with foreign Governments for the general settlement of Europe, and in the other took his personal share in the particular administration of his own country. It is to the former of these that our attention must be first directed.

To prevent any recurrence of those desolating wars which had just been terminated, it was determined to control France, the originator of the evil, by an armed occupation. The command of the force charged with this critical duty was intrusted by common consent to the Duke of Wellington, but for whose powerful mediation France would have fared far more hardly at the hands of the victorious Powers. The exasperated Prussians were bent upon demolishing the monuments of Paris; and even less revengeful spirits inclined to think that considerable concessions might be exacted from a nation which had inflicted such troubles and miseries on Europe at large. The Duke, however, restrained the fury of Blucher, and succeeded by the wisdom and force of his arguments in modifying the views of the allied Cabinets. It was owing to his representations and influence both that no penalty of confiscation was enforced against France, and that the occupation of her territory was temporary instead of permanent. Against the vindictiveness of some, the ambition of others, and the fears of more, he urged the incontrovertible plea that Europe could never be tranquil while France was agitated, and that France must infallibly be agitated if left with such reasonable ground of complaint. In all discussions of detail his opinion was invariably thrown on the side of moderation and indulgence, and though he abstained from interceding on behalf of Marshal Ney, it is hard to see how this omission can be designated as a dereliction of any positive obligations. It is certainly probable that a request from an officer in the Duke's position would not have been refused by the Government of France, but such a request the Duke was not bound to prefer by any considerations of duty or justice. It will hardly surprise the reader to learn that during his residence in the conquered capital his life was twice attempted by assassins —once when a quantity of gunpowder was placed in his cellars for explosion on the occasion of a fête, and, again, when a pistol was discharged at his carriage as he drove into the gates of his hotel. The author of this latter attempt was Cantillon, the miscreant to whom in respect of this very transaction, Napoleon bequeathed a pecuniary legacy.

In the year 1818 was held the first of those Royal *réunions* suggested by the political embarrassments to which we have alluded above. The King of Prussia and the Emperors of Austria and Russia met in the month of September at Aix-la-Chapelle, and this conference was attended on the part of the English Crown by the Duke of Wellington and Lord Castlereagh. The chief, if not the sole, public business here transacted was the agreement for the evacuation of France by the allied army, and the restoration of that State to its independent dignity among European nations. The proposal was in anticipation of the provisions of the treaty which had fixed five years as the possible term of occupation. The private interests of the Duke were largely concerned in the maintenance of this arrangement to its full extent. His position and emoluments as Generalissimo of the occupying force were exceedingly grand, and the inclination of most of his political colleagues tended, as he well knew, to the strict enforcement of the compact. Such considerations, however, had no weight against his impartial conclusions, and he so successfully exerted his influence in favour of France that the evacuation was decided upon without difficulty or delay.

In the several conferences which rapidly succeeded the meeting at Aix-la-Chapelle no part was taken either by England or her representatives; but in the year 1822 a congress was held at Verona, to which, as Plenipotentiary from the British Government, the Duke repaired, and the occasion is remarkable, not only from the results of the convention, but because it first identified the proceedings of the Duke with the debatable politics of the English Cabinet, and brought our military hero within the scope of Parliamentary animadversion. Among the subjects which the assembled Sovereigns regarded with anxious solicitude was the state of Spain. The Spanish people had peremptorily demanded the realization of those constitutional prospects with which they had long been beguiled, and it seemed probable that Ferdinand VII. would be compelled to yield. Such a compulsion was viewed at Verona in the light of a political sacrilege, and it was determined by France, with more or less assent on the part of the allied Crowns, to maintain the Royal prerogative in Spain by force of arms. It happened that just at this period the character of the British Cabinet had received its first important modification from the death of Lord Londonderry and the appointment of Mr. Canning to the Secretaryship of Foreign Affairs. The Duke, in fact, had received his instructions as Plenipotentiary from the pen of the new Minister, and when the actual invasion of Spain by a French army in support of absolutist principles was announced to the world, it was loudly exclaimed that either these instructions must have been disregarded, or that the Government had been grossly inattentive to its duty in permitting such an outrage upon the independence and liberties of a people. The debates in Parliament were long and violent, and though those were not times of Ministerial minorities the Opposition produced some impression by their protests. The Duke defended himself by proving what could never, of so strict a disciplinarian, have been seriously disbelieved—that he had faithfully conformed to his instructions, that those instructions included no authority to use menace, but that, as far as influence or remonstrance could go he had strongly dissuaded such interference with the affairs of the Spanish nation, and had set the difficulties of Peninsular intervention in the fullest light from his own experience. At this distance of time we can see that the affair, like many of our own day, was magnified beyond its due proportions for party purposes. It is not unreasonable to suspect that the Duke, who had no personal sympathies with Canning, and few, as yet, with his politics, may have co-operated somewhat ungraciously with the liberal successor of Castlereagh; but, apart from his invariable fidelity to his duties, it is perfectly certain, from his known opinions, that he must have been opposed to the renewal of war in the Peninsula under circumstances like these. He may have had very little affection for Spanish patriots, and he may have thought that the neutrality professed by his Government would have been as truly violated by contesting the decisions of Russia or France as by dictating terms to Spain, but his opposition to the project was doubtless exerted as cordially as his position allowed. With this occurrence terminated those peculiar duties of the Duke to which we have been referring; for, though he proceeded on a special embassy to St. Petersburgh in 1826, the event was not of a character to call for much remark.

During this participation in the counsels of Europe's rulers, the Duke invariably evinced that practical foresight which distinguished his character. He was not a liberal politician, nor what we might now term an enlightened statesman. He "had seen as much of war as most men," and most of the wars he had seen might be traceable, in his opinion, to the operation of democratic principles; but, if he was not in this respect very generously disposed, he was too wise and too sagacious to be tyrannical or severe. His experience of "constitutions," as devised by popular agitators, was not favourable. His principles inclined to legitimate monarchy and to "strong Governments," but none knew better than he that order could only be permanently maintained by consulting the wishes of the people as well as the caprices of the Sovereign, and his voice was given on the side of freedom, though not perhaps absolutely for freedom's sake.

It must not be imagined that England, during these proceedings, was forgetful of her hero. Honors, offices and rewards were showered on him from every quarter. As the Crown had exhausted its store of titles, and Parliament its forms of thanksgiving, the recognitions of his crowning victory took a more substantial shape. In addition to former grants, the sum of £200,000 was voted, in 1815, for the purchase of a mansion and estate to be settled on the dukedom. With these funds, a commission appointed for the purpose concluded a bargain with Lord Rivers for the noble domain of Strathfieldsaye, in Hampshire, to be held in perpetuity of the Crown by the Dukes of Wellington, on condition of presenting yearly a tri-colour flag to the British sovereign, on the 18th of June. This symbol, corresponding to a similar token presented by the Dukes of Marlborough, is always suspended in the Armory at Windsor Castle, where the little silken trophies may be seen hanging together in perpetual memory of Blenheim and Waterloo. The estate of Strathfieldsaye has since been largely increased by the investments of the Duke's private economy; it is now, we believe, many miles in circumference, and, though the mansion is not proportioned to the dignity either of the domain or the title, the avenue by which it is approached is almost unequalled. During the first year of his residence in Paris, the state of his health induced him to repair to Cheltenham, and gave occasion for an infinite number of grateful or festive acknowledgments. Among these was the opening of Waterloo Bridge, at which ceremony the hero of the title appeared, with the Prince Regent and the Duke of York, under a salute of 202 guns, and it was at the same period that the erection of the present Apsley House, a residence privately purchased by the Duke, was undertaken and completed by Mr. Wyatt. We are now so familiarized with monumental effigies of our hero in every possible guise, that it may surprise the reader to hear, that the trophy in the Park was for twenty years the only statue of the Duke of which the metropolis could boast. It was subscribed for by the ladies of England, between 1819 and 1821, and was erected on the Waterloo anniversary, in 1822, in which year, also, the merchants of London presented their elaborate shield. The crown, meantime, had lost no opportunity of signalizing its mindfulness of services rendered. The Duke, in 1818, was appointed Master-General of the Ordnance, in 1819 Governor of Plymouth, and in 1820 Colonel-in-Chief of the Rifle Brigade, into which, at the disbandment of certain regiments, the famous old 95th had been transmuted. As to foreign Courts, they had already said and done their utmost; but in 1818, the Sovereigns of Austria, Russia and Prussia simultaneously promoted the Duke to that rank in their respective forces which he had already reached in his own; so that of the soldier who has just expired, we may assert the incredible fact, that though he gained every honour by service and none by birth, he died a Field Marshal of near forty years standing in four of the greatest armies in the world.

The time, however, had now arrived when the great Duke was to take a more direct and visible part in the Administration of his country, and it was under the following circumstances that he entered on this duty. The old Tory Cabinet of the war had subsisted for ten years under the presidency of Lord Liverpool, without material modification in its constitution or policy. Mr. Canning, it is true, had been for some time at the head of the Board of Control, but it was not until his accession to the Foreign-office, in 1822, that his influence was substantially felt in the measures of the Govern ment. But now the elements of mighty change began perceptibly to work. The days of unmitigated Toryism were drawing to a close, and the precursors of reform appeared upon the scene. The principles of general liberalism in the person of Canning, and of free trade in that of Huskisson, were to be gradually introduced into the stubborn Cabinet of the Regency, and old men were at length to give place to new. Of the four ancient notabilities Lord Londonderry was already gone, Lord Sidmouth had just retired, Lord Eldon was declining, and the end of Lord Liverpool was at hand. It was a period of transition, and, like all such periods, was rife with angry suspicions, with incessant jars between the men of resistance and the men of progress, with mistakes, recriminations, compromises, and confessions.

Over and above the innumerable points of general

policy to be thus reconsidered, there were two great questions awaiting a decision—those of Parliamentary reform and Catholic emancipation. The former of these, though originally entertained by a Tory Minister, had become politically identified with the pledges of the Whigs, and was adopted rather than promoted by the "Radicals" of the time as the chief object of their agitation. The latter was less essentially a party question, for it concerned rather the practical government of Ireland than the recognition of a theoretical principle, and statesmen and Cabinets had been divided on its merits ever since the opening of the war. The measure, however, had been seized by the Whigs as their own; it had been defeated by the Tories, and its destinies were generally connected with the prospects of Whig ascendency. This party had now, for a very long interval, been excluded from power. Their adversaries had monopolized the credit of the war and the support of the electoral constituencies, and it almost seemed as if they were irremovably established in their seats of office.

During all this time the condition of the country had been disturbed and feverish in the extreme. Those public discontents which on the Continent had taken the form of military insurrection, in England assumed the shape of political agitation. George IV., who in 1820 had exchanged the title of Regent for that of King, was in no favour with the people. He had so long anticipated the position of Royalty, that his actual accession to the throne brought with it none even of those indefinite expectations which usually make a new reign popular. Though personally connected with the Whig party in times past, he had promptly confirmed the ascendency of the Tories on coming to the Crown; and the known selfishness of his disposition appeared to be only aggravated by power, while his more attractive qualities had gradually given place to the morosity of age. His personal character, indeed, figured largely in the complaints of the people, who described their Sovereign as absorbed in the luxurious enjoyments of a misanthropical seclusion while his subjects were suffering the extremities of pressure and want. There was great reason for these murmurs. Though the state of the country imperatively needed reforms, the great policy of the Ministry was that of repression alone. While new ideas were fermenting among the people with the diffusion of political knowledge and the growing conviction of misgovernment, the Cabinet policy was that of 20 years before, with its rigorous maxims of resistance and severity. The consequences were nothing but natural. The people were seduced by demagogues into wicked excesses and extravagant demands. They held nightly gatherings in the large towns and manufacturing shires, hatched chimerical plots of marching on the metropolis, talked plain treason at public assemblies, and proposed the forcible overthrow of the Government. A conspiracy for the assassination of the Ministry in a body was actually formed, and was not defeated by any want of resolution or earnestness on the part of the conspirators. On the other hand, the Government was confirmed by these very excesses both in its own repressive policy and in the support of the well-affected part of the population. They spared, therefore, neither the law nor the sword. They sent artillery into one county and special commissions into another; they charged public meetings with cavalry, and strung up rioters and sheepstealers on the same gallows. Their names were saluted with cries of execration, and their persons made the object of incessant hostility, but they paid spies to worm out the secrets of the seditious, and pursued their unswerving course in reliance on principles which had carried England, as they imagined, through worse storms than these.

In this unpopularity of the Administration the great Duke participated. Though it was impossible to overlook his transcendent claims to respect, and though he had not as yet taken any very active part in domestic politics, yet he was known to be of the Tory school, and connected, indeed, by ties of the closest sympathy with the hated Castlereagh. Even his military eminence was no recommendation in the eyes of those who denounced soldiers as the instruments of tyranny, and who had scarcely been brought, even by a galaxy of victories, to approve of an anti-democratic war. The indications, too, which he had given of his sentiments were not of a tendency to conciliate a suspicious public. As Master-General of the Ordnance he had taken a seat in the Cabinet, had concurred in the prosecution of the Queen, and had spoken in terms of soldierlike bluntness about certain proceedings of the Opposition. He was now, however, to do more. He was to become an influential member of the Administration, and to bear his part, for good or evil, in the important changes which were to convert the British Government from what it was under George IV. to what it is under Queen Victoria.

For two or three years affairs proceeded without the occurrence of any remarkable conjuncture. The foreign policy of England had been conclusively severed from that of the allied Courts of the Continent, and a few steps were taken in the direction of commercial emancipation; but the political crisis was still suspended. Mr. Canning and Mr. Huskisson were looked upon with no kindly eyes; but, though the wedge had been effectually inserted, no further impulse was given to it for some time. Lord Eldon croaked and prophesied, Lord Liverpool looked doubtingly ahead, and the Duke, perhaps, saw further than others; but the old Administration remained in outward form substantially the same, and the catastrophe was yet to come. At length, in February, 1827, Lord Liverpool's faculties suddenly failed him, and his fall left the Government not only without a head, but without that influence which had hitherto kept it together. Its constituents were divided among themselves on all the great questions coming on. The old shell of the Administration was anti-Catholic and anti-Liberal, but its vital elements represented emancipation and progress. The Duke had not yet discerned the necessity of the latter doctrines, but he was too sagacious to consort with dotards or bigots, and allied himself rather with Mr. Peel, who had succeeded to Lord Sidmouth's office of Home Secretary in 1822. Thus, besides the old Tory staff and the new leaven, there were the great Duke and his friends, who, if open to conviction, were not yet prepared for change, and by no means well disposed towards those who were promoting it.

At the time of Lord Liverpool's illness there were

two important subjects before the Legislature. The Roman Catholic question created a violent debate and a close division, while Mr. Huskisson's doctrines had taken the substantive form of a Corn Bill, intended to relax the restrictive system in force. The former subject came on under Canning's direction, while the government was still without a head; but the motion was lost in the Lower House, and was, consequently, not discussed in the Lords. After a few weeks, however, when if became evident that Lord Liverpool's recovery was beyond hope, the formation of a new Ministry became indispensable, and on the 10th of April the King sent for Mr. Canning. The claims of this statesman to the Premiership, both from official services and popular favour, were incontestable; but his opinions represented only a minority of the Cabinet, and it had now to be seen whether those who could co-operate with Mr. Canning under the conciliatory presidency of Lord Liverpool would be content to acknowledge his control as leader of the Administration. As far as Catholic emancipation went, no great difficulties need have intervened, for, though the new Premier's disposition in favour of Ireland was well known, the question was left an open one. But Mr. Canning, though not a Whig by profession, was a Liberal by principle, and his Ministry, under whatever title, must be a Liberal Ministry. For this the Duke was not prepared, and when the new appointment was duly communicated to the members of the late Government he, like the majority of his colleagues, sent in his resignation. Nor did he stop here, for he laid also at the King's feet the Master-Generalship of the Ordnance and the Commandership-in-

Chief, to which, at the Duke of York's death, he had naturally succeeded. Moreover, when in the ensuing June the Corn Bill of Canning and Huskisson came before the House of Lords, he moved and carried an amendment destructive of the measure, although it had been prepared by a government of which at the time he was a member.

These remarkable circumstances occasioned an extraordinary agitation in the public mind. It was asserted that the coincidence of the resignations, which all reached Mr. Canning within a few hours of each other, disclosed a combination of their writers against the independence of the Sovereign and the success of the new Administration, and as the Duke, though not the foremost statesman of the party, was the most distinguished personage concerned, and as he had taken what appeared to be the gratuitous step of retiring even from the Commandership-in-Chief, it was alleged that he had desired the Premiership for himself, and had adopted these measures to disconcert and embarrass the Government. On these points he delivered himself of an elaborate exculpation from his place in the House of Lords, averring, among other declarations, that, so far from seeking to conduct a Government, he was "sensible of being unqualified for such a situation," and that he "should have been mad to think of it"—words which were not forgotten in subsequent times. No reader will now suppose that the Duke of Wellington ever entertained the idea of dictating to his Sovereign, or of combining with others in the spirit imputed to him, nor is there, in fact, any need of such a forced hypothesis in explanation of the facts. What the Duke felt at the new appointment, all felt, and all were ready to mark their disapprobation. They did not desire a Liberal Government; they did not admire "political adventurers," and they were unprepared for a Cabinet in which the Premier was committed to the emancipation policy, however open the question might be considered. There is no doubt that, besides all this, the Duke was personally adverse to an intimate connexion with Mr. Canning, and this feeling induced him to discover hostility in the Premier's communications, and to decide against retaining an office which, though unpolitical in itself, would require a certain cordiality of co-operation with the head of the Government. As to his conduct on the Corn Bill, he disavowed amid angry bickerings any intention of annoying the Ministry, or even defeating the measure by the amendment which he suggested.

The whole episode was of brief duration. Exhausted by toil, deserted by those who should have supported him, and relentlessly persecuted by all who distrusted his politics or envied his elevation, Mr. Canning expired in the fourth month of his office, and left the King and the Government in worse perplexities than before. An Administration was then formed under Lord Goderich, who, as Mr. Robinson, had succeeded to the Chancellorship of the Exchequer at the time that Mr. Canning became Foreign Secretary. The new Cabinet closely resembled the last in its constitution, but its leader was wholly incapable of impressing any unity of purpose upon a Ministry in times like these .Mr. Canning died in August, and before the end of the year Lord Goderich had resigned his office in despair. Thus there appeared to be no chance of a good working Ministry under the Canning policy, while the true days of the old Tories were already past, and those of the Whigs not quite come. In his embarrassments the King did what Kings and Queens have so often done since; he sent for the Duke of Wellington. The Duke repaired to the Royal closet, and, to the surprise of some, the amusement of many, and the satisfaction of more, was gazetted as Prime Minister of England within eight months after his own declaration that the office was wholly beside his powers.

Since Canning's death he had so far qualified his recent secession from affairs as to return to the command of the army, and he had just gratified his countrymen by a series of visits to the aristocracy, in a progress which fell little short of the splendours of royalty. He was now to charge himself with the formation of a Cabinet and the responsible direction of public business, under circumstances found impracticable by those who had preceded him in the attempt. Perhaps both the King and the Duke would have preferred an Administration constructed wholly on the principles entertained by the Premier, but of this there appeared no acceptable chance. So the Duke took Mr. Huskisson, whom he misliked, and four more "Canningites" besides, but he still retained Peel at his side, and it was evident that the soul of the Administration resided here. The Chancellorship of the Exchequer was filled by Mr. Goulburn, a name long afterwards respectably connected with the party thus rising; but, though the Canningites formed the weaker element of the Cabinet, they were thought to contribute much towards shaping its policy; and so, in truth, they did, for, though the men were soon changed, their spirit survived in the measures brought forward.

Before the eyes of the great Duke and his colleagues there still loomed the three great questions of the time—questions on which neither all Liberals nor all Conservatives thought alike, but which the force of opinion was clearly pressing onwards for a decision. There was a question of religious disabilities, sometimes under the form of Corporation and Test Acts, but ultimately shaping itself into Irish Emancipation. There was the question of Free Trade, sometimes in the guise of Spitalfields or Navigation Acts, sometimes involved in corn averages or warehousing regulations, but always tending to untaxed bread; and finally, under motions for disfranchising one constituency and enfranchising another, appeared the mighty question of Parliamentary reform. On all these the Duke held opinions which were probably averse to material change. That he was opposed to the views of the Liberal party we cannot assert, for not all of the Liberal party desired the modification of the Corn Laws; nor that he was opposed to the wishes of the country, for the country on the whole, did not desire Catholic emancipation. But it is probable that, on his own judgment, he would have maintained the existing institutions in substantial integrity. What he then thought of the Corn Laws he had recently shown; what he thought, after much longer consideration, of Parliamentary reform, is not yet forgotten; and what he thought of religious disabilities we shall presently see.

The very first business of the session brought these principles on the table. Lord John Russell moved for a repeal of the Corporation and Test Acts—the first step towards that religious freedom which Catholic emancipation would manifestly consummate. Government opposed the measure; but the Reformers were too strong for them, and the measure was carried in a full house by a majority of 44. Moreover, although the Duke did not approve of this policy, there were some of his colleagues who did, so that he had to encounter with a divided Cabinet the declared resolution of the Commons. The times, indeed, were such that unanimity was scarcely attainable; for the old party could hold no longer, and no new formation had been made. These difficulties had demolished Lord Goderich, but they were not too great for the Duke, though his policy may at first sight appear not heroic. He yielded, took up the bill with a good grace, and, against the desperate resistance of his old friend Lord Eldon, and of all who thought the church and the constitution veritably at stake, carried it under his own auspices, through the House of Lords.

A month afterwards came a Corn Bill of Mr. Huskisson's again, and the Duke again compromised his private resolutions by accepting it as a Government measure. Later still, as if the session was to test the new Ministry on every vital point, the question of Parliamentary Reform was brought under discussion, upon a motion to disfranchise the two boroughs of Penryn and East Retford, and invest Manchester and Birmingham with the electoral privileges thus vacated. In the course of the contest, a division was taken on the particular substitution of Birmingham for East Retford. Government said "No" to the proposal, but Mr. Huskisson, though still Colonial Secretary, had managed to commit himself to an affirmative vote. Confused at his position, he sent the Duke what was either a resignation or an offer of resignation, and what the Duke chose to think was the former. There was, in plain truth, but little cordiality between them. Though the Duke's personal feelings had vanished with Mr. Canning's death, he had still no liking to his party, and certainly no preference for Mr. Huskisson above others. Unpleasant jars had occurred already. Mr. Huskisson had publicly assured his Liverpool constituents that he had not entered the new Administration without a "guarantee" for the general adjustment of its policy by that of Mr. Canning. This sounded as if a "pledge" had been exacted and given—an idea which the Duke indignantly repudiated; and Parliamentary explanations had to be offered before the matter could be set at rest. So this time the difference was made final. In vain did the common friends and colleagues of the two statesmen endeavour to "explain" the unlucky communication. The Duke, in terms which passed into proverbial use, replied, that there "was no mistake, could be no mistake, and should be no mistake." He was not sorry, in fact, that so convenient an opportunity had been created to his hand. Mr. Huskisson, therefore, retired, and with him retired not only Lord Dudley, Mr. Lamb, and Mr. Grant, but even Lord Palmerston. Of the Canningites, Lyndhurst alone remained; and the substitution of Lord Aberdeen, Sir Henry Hardinge, and Sir George Murray for the seceding malcontents at length gave consistency to the Wellington Ministry; and formed, with the names of Peel and

Goulburn, a party which has not perished yet. And what did the Duke now do with his solidified Cabinet and his unshackled policy? He gave up the principle of religious disabilities once and for all, and carried by main strength the great measure of Catholic emancipation!

This mighty question had now passed during a quarter of a century through all the vicissitudes of Parliamentary debate, The motions of the Grenville party and their followers between 1805 and 1812 had usually been defeated by majorities varying from 100 to 150 in the Commons, or still more decisive in the Lords. In the last-mentioned year Mr. Canning's proposals in favour of the Roman Catholics were lost by 129, but this majority had fallen below 50 in 1813. In 1821 the change was still more signally manifested. Mr. Plunkett actually carried a measure of concession through the Commons by a majority of 19, and Mr. Canning was equally successful in 1822, as was Sir F. Burdett in 1825; but the bills were, of course, lost in the Lords, though by smaller majorities than before. By this time, however, the Protestantism of the kingdom had taken the alarm; in 1827 a motion for a committee was lost, and in 1828 the opinions of the House seemed evenly balanced. It is not to be supposed that the measures here referred to suggested the absolute emancipation of the Roman Catholics. More or less liberal in their terms, they were usually tentative in character, and designed chiefly to secure the recognition of a principle on which enactments of substantial relief might be afterwards based. The circumstances of the discussion, too, had from time to time been seriously modified. Originally the question was considered in a light of such abstract policy that, as the Duke remarked, a bill concerning Roman Catholicism in England had been introduced into Parliament towards the close of the last century without even the knowledge of the authorities of Ireland. For a long time it was debated as involving points of principle alone, but of late years an agitation had been matured which metamorphosed the subject entirely. Instead of being a question of toleration, it was a question of government. To such a state had Ireland been brought by O'Connell and the priests, that Catholic emancipation was now demanded, not on the intrinsic merits of the claim, but as the sole means of satisfying a people not otherwise governable, and bringing one-third of the empire into harmony and unity with the rest. It was under this aspect that it exacted the attention of the Duke. Confident in their strength, and exasperated by the substitution of what they deemed an oppressive Ministry for the liberal and promising Cabinets of Canning and Goderich, the Irish confederates raged more furiously than before. They isolated themselves, as it were, from all the relations of political and social life for the one sole object of enforcing this demand upon the Government by a national movement. Ordinary crime was absorbed in this monster agitation, but there was no law but that of the priests, and no rule but that of O'Connell. At length he was even returned to Parliament for Clare, and it was proclaimed by an association, whose menace seemed warranted by its power, that every county in Ireland should record a like defiance of law and order.

It was upon these grounds,—the incurable anarchy of Ireland, the interminable division of Cabinets, the distraction of imperial councils, and the utter impossibility of maintaining such a state of affairs, that the Duke resolved on conceding to the Roman Catholics the emancipation they desired; nor can we now err in ascribing a material share in the decision to the co-operation of Robert Peel. There was no very cheering prospect before the two colleagues. That the influence of the Ministry and the example of the Duke would carry the measure, as a Government question, through the Legislature could hardly be doubted, but other and serious considerations were in the way. The Wellington Cabinet had been carried to power on the presumption, whether sound or otherwise, that they would maintain Protestant ascendency; this opinion was strongly felt by the electoral constituencies of the kingdom, and the conviction was generally understood to be shared in its fullest extent by the most exalted personage in the realm. Moreover, the question, though essentially one of progress, differed from all political questions of the like character in the reception it experienced among the people at large. Measures of pure political reform, however they may offend particular classes, are rarely unacceptable to the body of the nation; but when religious, instead of civil freedom, is at stake, the proposal seldom escapes some violent antagonism. In point of fact, it may be doubted to this day whether the majority of the people were ever really favourable to Catholic emancipation; so that Ministers, with all the pledges of their previous life against them, amid the reproaches of their former friends and the sarcasms of their new allies, were proposing to carry an almost unpopular measure under what appeared the intimidation of Irish terrorism. What the Duke, however, had once decided on doing he did most characteristically. In the first place, he resolved that there should be no compromise, insufficiency, or hesitation about the act itself. As concession was to be made, it should be made fully and freely, so as to satisfy all, and leave no rankling vestiges behind. In the next place, like a wise general, he gave his adversaries no opportunity of profiting by the disclosure of his plans, but kept his counsels to himself till the time came for action. Rumours escaped, as they always do, respecting the intentions of the Cabinet, but with little better foundation than the instinctive apprehensions of the Tories. Even the highest officers of the Crown were not all in the secret. The Attorney-General, Sir C. Wetherall, complained bitterly in the debate that his legal co-operation had been required only seven days before the opening of Parliament; and the Lord-Lieutenant of Ireland, the Marquis of Anglesey, publicly avowed his own want of information only six weeks earlier. Unfortunately, he did something more; he committed himself prematurely to the cause of the agitators; and, as the Duke suffered no such breaches of discipline, the indiscretion was followed by an instantaneous recall.

At length, however, on the 5th of February, 1829, the policy of the Government was plainly announced in the speech from the Throne; and when the field had been once taken the Duke made short work and sure. His Grace in the Upper House, and Mr. Peel in the lower, met the exigencies of their respective positions by manful acknowledgments and unanswerable reasoning. It was on this occasion that the Duke, having demonstrated the positive necessity of either advancing or receding, dismissed the latter alternative with his celebrated declaration :—"My lords, I am one of those who have probably passed more of my life in war than most men, and principally I may say in civil war too, and I must say this, that if I could avoid by any sacrifice whatever even one month of civil war in the coun try to which I am attached, I would sacrifice my life in order to do it." There was no rebutting such arguments, although the opposition was most determined; but the Duke carried his point, and in little more than a month the Relief Bill passed both Houses by large majorities, received the Royal assent, and became the law of the land.

Yet the success was not without its cost. Protestant societies wept over the "lost consistency" of the great Duke—the King was angered—Tories stood aloof from the Government—the Ministry was modified, and there was talk even of strengthening the Wellington Cabinet by the admission of Earl Grey. One episode of the history is too remarkable to be omitted. The Duke had been chosen patron of the new collegiate institution in the Strand, which, under the name of King's College, was destined to combat the rival seminary in Gower-street. On the disclosure of the Ministerial policy Lord Winchelsea, writing to a gentleman connected with the new establishment, spoke of the Duke and his patronship in these terms :—"Late political events have convinced me that the whole transaction was intended as a blind to the Protestant and High Church party, that the noble Duke, who had for some time previous to that period determined upon breaking in upon the constitution of 1688, might the more effectually, under the cloak of some outward show of zeal for the Protestant religion, carry on his insidious designs for the infringement of our liberties and the introduction of Popery into every department of the State." These expressions, coming from such a quarter, appeared to the Duke to call for personal notice, and after a vain essay of explanations, the Prime Minister of England, attended by Sir Henry Hardinge, and the Earl of Winchelsea, attended by Lord Falmouth, met in Battersea-fields on the 21st of March, in full session, to discharge loaded pistols at each other on a question concerning the Protestant religion. The life of the great captain, however, was not exposed to danger. Lord Winchelsea, after receiving the Duke's shot, fired in the air, and then tendered the apology in default of which the encounter had occurred.

What the Premier had now done in thus carrying this important measure could have been done by no other statesman in the kingdom. It was a feat which could never have been accomplished by a professed Liberal in opposition to the Tories, nor by any Tory, except one of high individual ascendency and strong personal resolution. Viewed merely as a Parliamentary performance it was a remarkable exploit, for great parties are not led from their old paths except under extraordinary conditions of influence and guidance. It is certain, however, that the result was immediately prejudicial to the public character of the Duke. He had not, indeed, yet sunk in that popular favour which always attends great conquerors, for his decisions had hitherto been all for Liberalism, and Liberalism is rarely offensive to the great mass of Englishmen. But with the upper and middle classes he had plainly lost ground, with the latter by his sacrifice of "Protestantism" and consistency—with the former by his irruption upon the old political traditions of government and party. In fact, the "strong Ministry" of the great Duke was already weak, partly from the disorganization of his supporters, partly from dislike of his military sternness, but mainly from the very nature of events and consequences. It had done its work; its one great object was accomplished, and, like the Ministry of 1846, after the repeal of the Corn Laws, it could do little better than retire with credit. But matters were not yet ripe for such a change, and the Duke, who perhaps hardly comprehended his own position, and who, if he had comprehended it, would never have weighed it against the position of the country, continued still to hold the reins of State.

Of the three great questions which the times were maturing for solution, the Duke, in his Ministerial capacity, had now practically disposed of two. In the matter of Free Trade he had given as much as was yet asked for, and in that of religious freedom he had even outstripped the desires of the public. But the third question, that of Parliamentary Reform, still remained for consideration, and it was upon this rock that his hitherto infallible sagacity was at length to make shipwreck. The subject had not been obscured even by the absorbing topic of the recent session. A Tory nobleman had even converted the Ministerial policy on the Emancipation Bill into an argument for the policy of the extreme Radicals, asserting, by a whimsical deduction, that purchasable seats could no longer be permitted to exist with safety, now that Papists might become the purchasers. To this singular proposal the old Reformers added their usual motions, but with so little success that even the moderate proposition, in which the Canningites concurred, of transferring to Birmingham the particular franchise of East Retford, was lost by a majority of 27. On the question of Parliamentary Reform, as comprehensively understood and agitated—that is to say, the systematic reconstruction of the people's House in the Legislature, Mr. Huskisson and his followers were of one mind with the Tories, nor had the Duke anything to apprehend in Parliament beyond the hopeless attempts of the purely liberal members. Perhaps, if he had seen symptoms of greater urgency out of doors, he might have corrected his opinion; but, in point of fact, public agitation, though so violent a few months later, did not wear a very serious aspect at the opening of 1830. Political unions—those leagues which afterwards became so famous—had been instituted in some large towns, but with the object, as it appeared, of their own special enfranchisement rather than of any general innovations. The great change in the national mind was wrought or precipitated by the effect of an example, and this example was close at hand.

In the summer of the year 1830 Europe once more experienced the shock of a French revolution—a shock which was transmitted instantaneously from the Seine to the Vistula, and which this time lost little of its force in crossing the British Channel. Its operation was greatly facilitated by a demise of the Crown. George IV. had expired just at this period, and with him had gone all that the Tories relied on and the Liberals feared, in the personal influence of the Sovereign. On his throne there was now seated an affable and conciliatory Monarch, known to be generously inclined, and believed to be well disposed towards the advocates of constitutional reforms. He had acted like his predecessor in confirming the existing Ministry in office, and he had even been at pains to dispel a prevalent assumption of his personal dislike to the Premier. But the plot was now thickening rapidly, and events for once left the great Duke behind. Throughout the length and breadth of the land there spread rapidly a feverish sympathy with the French, an ardent desire for improved institutions, and a resolute determination to attain an end, however imperfectly conceived. The Duke did not comprehend this movement, and, as he was not for it, he was against it. He could not tolerate disorder, and so he turned to measures of repression. He had committed himself by injudicious proceedings against the press, and he now damaged his credit still further by his attitude of unyielding and peremptory resistance to public feeling. At the present moment of national regret it will hardly appear credible that England's hero should ever have fallen into such popular disesteem as was then exhibited, but the conjuncture was exceptional, and circumstances combined strangely against his credit with the nation. He had offended his old colleagues by his Liberalism and his new allies by his Conservatism; he had scandalized "stanch Protestants"—never an uninfluential portion of the community—by surrendering his position; and he was now to offend the unreasoning multitude by making a stand. Besides this, he was connected in popular rumours with the obnoxious Polignac, whom he was said to have abetted in his tyrannical attempts, and whose proceedings unluckily resembled his own in respect of his treatment of the press. Even the professional renown of the great captain rather injured than helped him at this gloomy crisis, for he was regarded as the personification of that force which might be employed against liberty, to the possible destruction of popular hopes. Stories went abroad of military preparations, special musters, and significant appointments, and even the cleansing of the Tower ditch, under the directions of the Duke as Constable of that fortress, though suggested simply by the removal of Old London-bridge, was represented as a menace against the citizens of London. Though twenty years of better feeling have since elapsed, it is not without shame that we record the ebullitions of discontent which ensued. It was pretended that the Duke's life would not be safe in the city at the Lord Mayor's feast, and it is certain that the conqueror of Waterloo was hooted through Piccadilly, and that the windows of his residence were protected against his own countrymen by casings of iron.

The Whigs now saw that their time was come, nor did the Duke refuse the battle. He knew that the fight was for Parliamentary Reform, and he brought the point to an issue without the delay of an hour. It surprises observers of our own generation to conceive how such a man at such a crisis could ever have been so mistaken. To all appearances the conjuncture of affairs fell pecuiarly within the range of his statesmanship. It was a question of yielding, or resisting, of assigning a due and proper value to the reality of the grievance, the demands of the times, and the force of opinion. The Duke had understood such questions in the cases of Free Trade and Catholic Emancipation, and it is astonishing that he should have stumbled at a case which was clearer than either. To us it seems that the justice of the popular demand, the urgency of the crisis, and the probable safety of the experiment, ought to have been as clear to the Duke's eyes at that time as they are to our own at present. None could read signs around him better than he, and yet for this once he utterly failed. The new Parliament met in November, and at the very opening of the session the Duke delivered his memorable declaration, "that the country already possessed a Legislature which answered all the good purposes of legislation, that the system of representation possessed the full and entire confidence of the country, and that he was not only not prepared to bring forward any measure of reform, but would resist such as long as he held any station in the Government of the country." These few words decided in five minutes the destinies of the Government and the country too. Radical reform became an immediate certainty, and away went the Tories for ever, and the Wellington party for ten long years.

Thus terminates the great Duke's Ministerial career. When his party, after so protracted an eclipse, reappeared in 1841 under the new title of "Conservatives," he resumed, indeed, his place in the Cabinet, but without special office or active political duty. From this time his capacity in the Administration of the State acquired those peculiar features with which we are now so familiar. Without being professionally a member of Government, his aid was understood to be always available for Ministerial Councils, and the command of the army, which he had resigned on accepting the Premiership, but which had reverted to him in 1843, supplied a pretext, if any were wanting, for investing him with this exceptional function. Perhaps no position could have been better suited to his political abilities. That he was not a great statesman in the proper acceptation of the term, we need not scarcely remark; and he evinced, in fact, no less than his usual sagacity when from his seat in Parliament he made the candid but exaggerated avowal of his incompetence for high civil office. The declaration was apparently contradicted by subsequent events, but it was, in reality, founded upon sound self-knowledge and a distinct perception of affairs. It is quite true that at a conjuncture when measures seemed less important than men, and when, from the decline of the Tories, the abeyance of the Whigs, and the death of Canning, there was an absolute void in the political world, the King sent for the Duke, and made him Prime Minister of England. But it certainly cannot be said that his performances in this position belied his own anticipations, or proved him more fit than he had believed himself to conduct the government of a State like England. He displayed certain abilities, beyond doubt, and did, as we have said, what no other man could have done at the time. It was plain, however, that he was no longer in his proper element. The Wellington of Downing-street was not the Wellington of Portugal.

He could take sound views of most subjects before him, and carry out a Government resolution with unflinching promptitude. He could amuse the country by his application of regimental discipline to the lounging clerks of his offices, and set a more important example by introducing military economy into the management of public business. But for the higher and more comprehensive duties of a statesman he had not been trained, perhaps not born, and none saw the truth more clearly than himself. What he had intended to assert was, that he felt himself unqualified for the professional exercise of those high civil powers, in the contention for which many of those around him had spent the studies and experience of a life. This simple statement he expressed, according to his custom, in hyberbolical terms, to which occurrences almost immediately ensuing supplied a somewhat whimsical contradiction; but the truth had been spoken nevertheless. Now, however, he was released from the responsibilities of which he felt incompetent, and called upon for nothing but those sage opinions which on particular subjects were of such unquestioned value. In this capacity he was by no means illiberally disposed. He had seen too many parties broken up, and had taken too great a share in the work himself, to be bigotedly attached to party distinctions, and the course of events towards the close of his career tended still more completely to obliterate those political landmarks which had existed at the beginning. The Duke, therefore, though a Conservative by descent and tradition, was no violent antagonist of the Whigs. He knew that "the Queen's government must be carried on," and this government could be carried on much more smoothly with his co-operation than under the disapproval, however tacit, of so distinguished a subject. So he did the best in his power for all, discharging his duties with nearly the same cordiality whether a Whig or a Tory Premier was at the helm, and regarding the general efficacy of the State machinery as a more important consideration than the traditions of the party in power. If he was not one of "Her Majesty's advisers" by office, he was incontestably so in fact, for no character of history was ever summoned more frequently to give counsel to royalty in straits. Whether the embarrassment was a sudden resignation of the ministry, or an imperfect conception of an Administration, or a Bedchamber plot, or a dead lock, it was invariably the Duke who was called in—sometimes as a man who could do and say to others of all ranks and parties what could be said and done by no other person living, sometimes as an arbiter in whose decision all disputants would concur, sometimes as a pure political fetish to get the State out of trouble, nobody could tell how.

Arguments had been devised to prove that in carrying the Catholic Relief Bill the Duke of Wellington was but developing the principles professed in the Irish Parliament by Arthur Wesley. We cannot attach any value to such deductions. There is little room for mistake about the Duke's political conduct. He had no conception whatever of enfranchisement for freedom's sake. He did not like the repeal of the Test Acts, but he accepted it as a necessity when the times were too strong for him. At his own Relief measure he never looked as Wilberforce looked on the Abolition Act, or

Lord Grey on the Reform Bill. In his eyes it was no triumph of principle—it was a "bad business," as he plainly said, but "the State was aground." All that can be said is, that he recognized necessity when it arrived, and made the best of it, like a soldier. If he would fain have maintained these oppressive statutes, he did not, at any rate, conceive that the absolute existence of the Church and the Constitution was contained in them, and, if he did the work of repeal with reluctance, he at least did it not negligently. The characteristics of his policy must be sought, not in the principle of the great measure he was proposing—for at heart he condemned it—but in the tactics by which he carried it through the Legislature. He knew that if it was to be done there was but one way to do it, and he took it out of the people's hands into his own. He breathed not a syllable of his purpose till the action had commenced, and he then brought the whole force of Government upon the point without scruple or delay. His adversaries clamoured loudly against both his concealment and his precipitation—a sure proof of the sagacity in which the plan was conceived. He knew that if he had given time for an "appeal to the country" the country would very probably have gone wrong, and, after he had once seen what was right, he took the whole responsibility of the decision upon himself.

From this period the Duke's time passed smoothly enough along. His transient unpopularity speedily vanished with the decline of agitation and his own presumed return to a more reasonable policy. The people soon forgot that he had been an obstructive, and the Tories that he had been a Repealer. He was soon cheered in the streets again as "the great Duke," and when the University of Oxford, in 1834, elected him its Chancellor, we may fairly consider that his compulsory Liberalism had been condoned. In the same year it seemed for a moment as if his Ministerial life were to recommence, and under singular conditions too. The Whigs had been dismissed, and the King, as usual, "sent for the Duke." The Duke advised that Sir Robert Peel should be charged with the formation of a Ministry, but Sir Robert was abroad, and until his return, therefore, the Duke actually, at his Sovereign's desire, took upon himself *ad interim* eight of the chief Government offices together, including those of the three Secretaries of State. In one of the latter—that of Foreign Affairs—he was induced to remain; but in a few weeks the whole fabric vanished, and there was an end of the hazard till 1841. And now, as time and circumstances were gradually levelling the distinctions of party, the Duke's business became easier still. True to his own creed, he accepted the definite repeal of the Corn Laws, and under the same conditions, indeed, would probably have proposed it. He had no longer much difficulty in adjusting himself to Conservative Whigs or Liberalized Tories. His rule was necessity—and most Governments of late years have been guided by the Duke's own standard.

In turning, however, to the military character of the hero who has just expired, we shall be under no necessity of modifying the eulogies which all Englishmen will desire to hear. In pronouncing the great Duke to have been one of the most consummate generals ever known, we can run no risk of being led into exaggeration by our gratitude or our regret. The opinion must be confirmed by the voice of history, for there is no test of military excellence which the Duke's achievements will not sustain. He was victorious against all kinds of enemies and in all kinds of warfare. He circumvented Asiatics more deceitful than the Affghans, and subjugated races more powerful than the Sikhs. His campaign of Waterloo was briefer and more brilliant than that of Jena, and his seven years' war in the Peninsula was maintained without the reverses and with more than the successes of Frederick the Great. The troops which he conquered were those which had previously conquered all the troops of Europe in succession; the generals who failed before him were those whom no other commanders had been able to resist. If it be said that there were soldiers against whom Wellington was never pitted, yet these had been already beaten by those whom he surpassed, so that the first place was clearly the right of England's Duke alone. He showed himself master of defensive tactics in Portugal, of offensive tactics in Spain, of mountain warfare in the Pyrenees, of strategy at Salamanca, of true military science everywhere. His forecast was unfailing, and if his operations ever suffered for lack of provision the fault is invariably traceable to those who had neglected his warnings. To say that he was overcautious or phlegmatic is to speak in total ignorance of his exploits. His position in the Peninsula did not admit of the license assumed by generals who had free privilege to rob and unbounded command of reinforcements; but never was a battle won with a more reckless dash than that of Assaye, never a feat of arms more audacious than the passage of the Douro, never a campaign more rapid or brilliant than that which carried the British army from the Agueda to the Garonne.

Nor was his genius less eminently conspicuous in the manufacture of his materials. The Duke made his own army, and with few aids beyond the school of the militia and the reminiscences of Egypt. Yet, before the Spanish war had reached its second campaign, Napoleon drew out for the use of his generals a new scheme of tactics to be employed against "*good troops*, like the English." To such a point, too, had the excellence of the Portuguese army been brought under his vigilant supervision, that at the opening of the campaign of 1815, when hard pressed for troops on whom he could rely, he had applied, though in vain, for the aid of his old Peninsular contingent on the plains of the Netherlands. That he was beloved by the army to the extent which his victories might have warranted is more than can be said. In those qualities which conciliate personal affection he was naturally deficient. He always and inflexibly considered duty before feeling, and put nothing in the balance against the rules of the service, the needs of the Government, and the general good of the State. On the question of the Peninsular medals it was not unreasonably thought that he sacrificed substantial claims on his advocacy to notions of official punctilio. But if he rarely tempered his duties with kindness, he always performed them with consideration, and never permitted them to be affected by interest or favour. If not generally loved, he was universally respected, admired, and confided in. He certainly never possessed Cæsar's power of fascination, and yet the Peninsular army, as we are emphatically told by its historian, felt to him as the 10th legion felt towards Cæsar. He was always mindful of their professional wants, always jealous of their honour, and, above all, he invariably conducted them to victory.

There are two great commanders—one of a past age and one of our own, with whom it may be natural, if not profitable, to compare the third, who has just departed. Between the careers of Wellington and Marlborough there are these points in common—that both appeared on the scene at the beginning of a century when the overgrown power of France was threatening Europe with subjection; that both found the military credit of England at its lowest point, and that both succeeded by their victories and conquests in raising it to the highest. Both were crippled by the fetters of a coalition and the necessities of a Government; both worked with inadequate means, and both brought their wars to a triumphant conclusion. But with these superficial similarities the resemblance ends. In no personal capacity can Wellington be likened to Marlborough. The latter, a dissolute and unprincipled courtier, with no visible quality of a soldier beyond title and costume, suddenly found himself when already Knight of the Garter, Duke, and Captain-General of England, intrusted through private interests with the command of an army. In this situation he developed, apparently without consciousness to himself, the intuitive genius of an unrivalled general, exactly as if the dæmon of military genius had suddenly possessed himself of the body of a fop. On the other hand, Wellesley, a younger brother, with no fortune but his sword, and little more aid from interest than was then absolutely required for common promotion, fighting his way upward step by step, and receiving no rank which was not due to his services, whatever might have actually been the motives for its bestowal, won his command at last rather by force of merit than help of favour. To this training his military qualities corresponded. Without enthusiasm, affectation, or hypocrisy, he set steadily to work upon his purpose, overlooking no conditions which might influence the result, making the best of his means, and hoping the best of his fortune. His capacity seems to have differed from that of his contemporaries rather in degree than in kind. He was not a heaven-born general, but he possessed all the distinctive qualities of English officers in greater excellence than any of them. It appears to have been his conviction that war depended for its success rather upon the unceasing exertions of sound military practice than the eccentric strokes of genius. He was not wanting in either enterprise or audacity, for audacity and enterprise occasionally furnish the most prudent principles of action, but in general he relied rather on those calculations of experience which rarely deceive; and though he has been styled the favourite of fortune by writers driven to seek some consoling explanation of his victories, he in reality trusted less to fortune than any general ever known. He measured his own strength, and that of his antagonists, with the most unerring nicety, and computed distant results with a sagacity which has rarely been equalled. His conclusions were of universal application, for they were founded on observation and formed with impartiality.

While outnumbered and overmatched in Portugal, and destined, in men's estimation, to speedy discomfiture, he was speculating correctly on the Imperial system of Napoleon, and supplying the English Ministry with plans of operation in Canada, Sicily, or Sweden. He comprehended, in short, the true situation of Europe, military as well as political, when the like knowledge had not been attained by any other living man.

If, again, we couple the names of Wellesley and Bonaparte, we shall find the materials rather for a contrast than a parallel. Their opportunities, their means, and their objects were widely different. To argue from the victory of Waterloo that Wellington was a greater General than Napoleon would be merely to adopt a fallacy of popular judgment; but we see no reason for concluding that Bonaparte would have fared better than his marshals in that protracted struggle which tried the military power of the two nations. As Wellington's successes increased the impatient Emperor did, indeed, announce his intention from time to time, of descending upon the Tagus to "finish the war with a clap of thunder," and he censured the errors of his marshals with equal particularity and vehemence. But it is hard to see what more he could have done himself beyond extinguishing their ill-timed rivalries by the predominant force of his will. The French armies could hardly have received any material augmentation, for the Peninsula was already saturated with the Imperial legions; nor could they have been concentrated in much larger masses for much longer periods, since the country, as was proved, could not maintain them. No one, we presume, will assert, that the Emperor could have conducted the Portuguese invasion more resolutely than Massena, or plunged into the Pyrenees more audaciously than Soult. He would never, it is true, have overlooked an opportunity, but the British general would never have given him one. Napoleon owed much to the weakness of his antagonists, but Wellington was neither a Mack nor a Benningsen, nor an Alexander, nor a Frederick William, nor even an Archduke Charles. At Waterloo, and there, perhaps, only, Napoleon on a fair field encountered really good troops, handled by a really great commander, and then he failed.

We may admit, without derogation to the claims of our national hero, that he might perhaps have been unequal to those gigantic combinations by which Napoleon extended the Imperial sway from Sweden to Sicily, and from the Bay of Biscay to the Niemen. Possibly no man but Napoleon could have conceived and executed, in the nineteenth century such a scheme of universal empire. But Bonaparte worked by prodigies, and Wellington by ordinary means. One exercised absolute and irresponsible dominion over a mighty nation of soldiers, and disposed at his discretion of contingents from two-thirds of Europe. The other could barely obtain an army of 30,000 men, and in the command of these he was fettered by jealous restrictions, annoyed by factious complaints, and crippled by the want of necessary supplies. Napoleon's marshals might rob, massacre, and terrify at pleasure—they owed no account to their master on any score but that of success. Wellington was compelled by position, no less than policy, to conciliate instead of coercing, nor is it too much to say, that half the energies which should have been disposable against the enemy were consumed in expostulations with his countrymen and allies. The military powers of the two commanders were never brought fairly to a contest. All we can say is, that Wellington's prognostications of the soundness of his own system, as compared with Napoleon's, were verified to the letter, and that what could be done with 50,000 troops against a million, was done by the British general. He took post in a craggy corner of the continent, and there maintained himself against all the strength and all the science that could be despatched to subdue him. Waiting his opportunity, he at length issued from his retreat, and continued his victorious course over the borders of France. He was once, at a period which would have brought him face to face with the great Emperor, offered a command in Germany, and the result might have solved the question which it is now profitless to debate. His reply was so characteristic of his plain sense and modesty, that we subjoin it as it was given: "I am the Prince Regent's servant, and I will do whatever he and his Government please. But I would beg of them to recollect that the great advantages which I enjoy here, consist in the confidence that everybody feels that I am doing what is right, which advantage I should not enjoy, for a time at least, in Germany. Many might be found to conduct matters as well as I can, both here and in Germany; but nobody would enjoy the same advantage here, and I should be no better than another in Germany." An attentive student of the German campaigns might be inclined, perhaps, on this point, to doubt the great

Duke's conclusion. His part would have been surely played even in such composite battles as that of Leipsic; and since Napoleon never commanded a better army, and Wellington could hardly have had a ruder one, than those which fought at Waterloo, it is natural to draw from this engagement some inferences applicable to a campaign.

Both Wellington and Napoleon, like most great generals, were eminently endowed with administrative talents, and both conceived themselves peculiarly gifted in matters of finance. The Duke is even said to have expressed his opinion that his true genius was rather for the Exchequer than the War-office. At one of the most critical conjunctures of the Peninsular War he drew up a most able paper on the true principles of Portuguese banking; and at Seringapatam, after very serious evils had been experienced from a long standing debasement of the coinage, a memorandum was accidentally discovered in the treasury from the pen of Colonel Wellesley, every prediction and observation of which had been exactly verified by events. On this point, no less than on the question of military strategy, the gigantic scale on which the French Emperor acted precludes any effective comparison with operations in a smaller sphere. It would be ridiculous to question Napoleon's extraordinary genius for organization in the face of such imperishable records as remain. But in estimating these creations his unparalleled facilities of action should be taken into account. With no opinions to consult, no interests to reconcile, no claims to adjust—with a *tabula rasa* of all rights, prejudices, institutions, and establishments, it was not very difficult for a creative genius to occupy itself with the task of constructing anew. Wellington enjoyed no such opportunities. His abilities were tasked in a Government where all progress is the result of compromise, where no interest is destroyed without compensation, where the most resolute Minister is forced to qualify his own convictions in deference to those of his opponents, and where every act has to sustain the tedious ordeal of Parliamentary discussion. We do not say that Wellington possessed Napoleon's power of administration. We are aware that no such pretensions could be advanced on his behalf. But it should be also added that their respective spheres of action admit of no comparison, and that the Duke's conclusions if less brilliant than the conceptions of his antagonist, have proved better calculated for the test of experience.

The chief characteristic of Wellington's mind was that sterling good sense which is said to distinguish the capacities of his countrymen in general. This peculiar merit is visible in every line of his despatches and in every act of his career. He never neglected opportunities of observation. While stopping at Madras, on his first voyage to Calcutta, he so acquainted himself with the administration of that Presidency that the Mysore war found his local knowledge already prepared. Before hostilities commenced with Scindiah, he had studied the features of the debateable ground, and drawn up minutes on the management of a Mahratta campaign. He was found prepared, when the emergency arrived, with memoranda for operations in Egypt, in Portugal, and in Spain. He gave advice to Louis and Ferdinand, which, if followed, might have saved many of the revolutions he lived to see. He was never credulous nor enthusiastic, bigoted nor vindictive. He restrained the exasperation of Blucher in 1815, and threw his weight, as we have seen, on the side of moderation in the councils of Vienna. He never set human nature at more or less than it was worth. He made allowance for passions, interests, and contingencies, computed things at their true value, and deduced conclusions which were rarely wrong. His despatches abound with opinions of the Governments, politics, and men with whom he was brought into contact; and it would be difficult to point out one among them all which facts have not more or less confirmed.

The long period of peace which it has been the fortune of our generation to experience gave the great Duke no opportunity of again displaying his talents in the field, but he still, as Commander-in-Chief of the British army, contributed the benefits of his unmatched ability to the military administration of the country. He had once, as we have seen, either from caprice, or punctilio, resigned this office, at the time of Mr. Canning's Premiership, and he again relinquished the charge in 1828, as incompatible with his own position as Mr. Canning's successor. In 1843, however, on the death of Lord Hill, he resumed the command of the forces, which he retained till his death. His general views in this capacity partook of his policy at large. His administrative talent was incontestable, and was evinced by the order and economy of every department under his charge, and the effective working of the whole. On all points of discipline his regulations were distinguished by a perfect knowledge of the characters with which he had to deal, and by that sound common sense which never forsook him. As respected the organization and equipment of the army, no opinions could be more liberal than his own; but it cannot be said that he was equally enlightened in his views of the service in general. In fact, he looked upon military reforms as he looked upon civil reforms, without absolute bigotry, but with no willing mind. The successive improvements in the condition of the British soldier originated with others than the Commander-in-Chief, and were not unusually carried out in his despite. For all that could make the soldier "efficient," according to the old practical ideas of efficiency, a ready advocate was always to be found in the Duke; but the reforms of the recruiting and the relief systems, the amelioration of barrack life, and the abolition of military flogging, were not due to the Commander-in-Chief, though experience has now shown with what perfect propriety they were introduced. His professional faculties never failed him to the last. His views respecting the exposure of our coasts to invasion, however their soundness might have been contested at the time, were indisputably correct according to the maxims of his own experience. If there was error, it was not in judgment, but in understanding. If Frenchmen and Englishmen were indeed such as the Duke had known them—if war was to be, as heretofore, the appeal of Kings and Cabinets at the first international disagreement—then there could be no doubt that our defences were inadequate for public security. These conditions we may hope have somewhat changed, but it can be little reproach to the old Duke that he had not yet arrived at such conviction. On our famous 10th of April, his peculiar genius was exerted to the unspeakable advantage of peace and order. So effective were his preparations that the most serious insurrection could have been successfully encountered, and yet every source of provocation and alarm was removed by the dispositions adopted. No military display was anywhere to be seen. The troops and the cannon were all at their posts, but neither shako nor bayonet was visible, and for all that met the eye, it might have been concluded that the peace of the metropolis was still intrusted to the keeping of its own citizens. As an instance, however, of his forecast against the worst on this memorable occasion, it may be observed that orders were given to the commissioned officers of artillery to take the discharge of their pieces on themselves. The Duke knew that a cannon shot too much or too little might change the aspect of the day, and he provided by these remarkable instructions both for imperturbable forbearance, as long as forbearance was best, and for unshrinking action, when the moment for action came.

In the House of Lords the Duke was a regular attendant and not unfrequently a speaker, but the journals of that august body supply few testimonies of our hero's excellence. His opinions and votes, excepting when his natural Conservatism had not yet been sufficiently influenced by pressure from without, were rarely otherwise than soundly given, but his motives were often imperfectly expressed. It has been said that a collection of Cromwell's speeches would make the most nonsensical book in the world, and though such a remark is certainly not warranted by the orations of Wellington, yet in this point a certain resemblance is discoverable between the two great soldiers. The Duke allowed himself, in addressing the House, to be carried away, not perhaps by his feelings, but by the impetus of a delivery which, without being either fluent or rapid, was singularly emphatic and vehement. He magnified his own opinions in order to impress them upon his hearers. If he recommended, as he did with great alacrity, a vote of thanks to an Indian general, the campaign was always "the most brilliant he had ever known;" if he wished to stigmatize a disturbance of the peace, it was something transcending "anything he had ever seen in all his experience," though such a quality could hardly be predicated of any disorders under the sun. One of the best chroniclers of his deeds has attributed this precipitate bestowal of praise and censure to a natural failure of character, but we suspect that in many cases the error of the opinion was due to the manner of its delivery alone. Few men have been intrusted with more delicate missions in the distribution of rewards, and none could have discharged such duties with more unimpeachable discrimination. The Duke could appreciate events with unfailing nicety, but he failed in the capacity to describe them, and of late years his speeches, where they were not tautology, were often contradictions. Nor could the failing be traceable to age alone, for it was observed, though in a less degree, during the earlier stages of his career, and is the more remarkable from the contrast presented by his despatches. No letters could ever be more temperately or perspicuously expressed than these famous documents. Even as specimens of literary composition they are exceedingly good—plain, forcible, fluent, and occasionally, like those of Napoleon, even humorous withal. It is true that the correspondence, especially in the earlier volumes, often partakes of a more familiar character than pertains to a general's "despatches;" but if the reader desires to feel the full force of our encomium we need only refer him to the despatches of Marlborough for a subject of comparison.

The private life of the Duke was simple, methodical and familiar in most of its features to all inhabitants and visitors of the metropolis. His attendance at the early service at the Chapel Royal and at the Whitehall sermons, his walk in the park in former years, and of late times his ride through the Horse Guards, with his servant behind him, are incidents which every newspaper has long chronicled for the information of the country. His personal habits were those of military punctuality, his daily duties were discharged systematically as they recurred, and his establishment was as thriftily regulated as the smallest household in the land. This economy enabled him to effect considerable savings, and it is believed that the property of the title must have been very largely increased. He married in 1806 the Hon. Catharine Pakenham, third daughter of the second Baron Longford—a lady for whose hand, as Arthur Wellesley, with nothing but the sword of an infantry captain to second his pretensions, he had previously, we are informed, been an unsuccessful suitor. The Duchess died in 1831, and the Duke's name was recently coupled with that of numerous ladies who were successively selected by report as the objects of his second choice. He expired, however, a widower, leaving two sons to inherit his name. Full of years beyond the term of mortality, and of honours almost beyond human parallel, he has descended into his grave amid the regrets of a generation who could only learn his deeds from their forefathers, but who know that the national glory which they witness and the national security which they enjoy were due, under God's providence, to the hero whom they have just now lost.

THE TIMES' 'LEADER' ON THE DEATH OF THE DUKE.*

If aught can lessen this day the grief of England upon the death of her greatest son, it is the recollection that the life which has just closed leaves no duty incomplete and no honour unbestowed. The Duke of WELLINGTON had exhausted nature and exhausted glory. His career was one unclouded longest day, filled from dawn to nightfall with renowned actions, animated by unfailing energy in the public service, guided by unswerving principles of conduct and of statesmanship. He rose by a rapid series of achievements which none had surpassed to a position which no other man in this nation ever enjoyed. The place occupied by the Duke of WELLINGTON in the councils of the country and in the life of England can no more be filled. There is none left in the army or the Senate to act and speak with like authority. There is none with whom the valour and the worth of this nation were so incorporate.

* This was the only editorial article of the Times of September 15, 1852.

Yet, when we consider the fulness of his years and the abundance of his incessant services, we may learn to say with the Roman orator, "*Satis diu vixisse dicito*," since, being mortal, nothing could be added either to our veneration or to his fame. Nature herself had seemed for a time to expand her inexorable limits, and the infirmities of age to lay a lighter burden on that honoured head. Generations of men had passed away between the first exploits of his arms and the last counsels of his age, until, by a lot unexampled in history, the man who had played the most conspicuous part in the annals of more than half a century became the last survivor of his contemporaries, and carries with him to the grave all living memory of his own achievements. To what a century, to what a country, to what achievements was that life successfully dedicated! For its prodigious duration—for the multiplicity of contemporary changes and events, far outnumbering the course of its days and years—for the invariable and unbroken stream of success which attended it from its commencement to its close, from the first flash of triumphant valour in Indian war to that senatorial wisdom on which the SOVEREIGN and the nation hung for counsel to its latest hour—for the unbending firmness of character which bore alike all labour and all prosperity—and for unalterable attachment to the same objects, the same principles, the same duties, undisturbed by the passions of youth and unrelaxed by the honours and enjoyments of peace and of age—the life of the Duke of WELLINGTON stands alone in history. In him, at least, posterity will trace a character superior to the highest and most abundant gifts of fortune. If the word "heroism" can be not unfairly applied to him, it is because he remained greater than his own prosperity, and rose above the temptations by which other men of equal genius, but less self-government, have fallen below their destinies. His life has nothing to gain from the language of panegyric, which would compare his military exploits or his civil statesmanship with the prowess of an ALEXANDER or a CÆSAR, or with the astonishing career of him who saw his empire overthrown by the British General at Waterloo. They were the offspring of passion and of genius, flung from the volcanic depths of revolutions and of civil war to sweep with meteoric splendour across the earth, and to collapse in darkness before half the work of life was done. Their violence, their ambition, their romantic existence, their reverses, and their crimes will for ever fascinate the interest of mankind, and constitute the secret of their fame, if not of their greatness. To such attractions the life and character of the Duke of WELLINGTON present no analogy. If he rose to scarce inferior renown, it was by none of the passions or the arts which they indulged or employed. Unvanquished in the field, his sword was never drawn for territorial conquest, but for the independence of Europe and the salvation of his country. Raised by the universal gratitude of Europe and of this nation to the highest point of rank and power which a subject of the British monarchy could attain, he wore those dignities and he used that influence within the strictest limits of a subject's duty. No law was ever twisted to his will, no right was ever sacrificed by one hair's breadth for his aggrandizement. There lived not a man either among his countrymen or his antagonists who could say that this great Duke had wronged him; for his entire existence was devoted to the cause of legal authority and regulated power. You seek in it in vain for those strokes of audacious enterprise which in other great captains, his rivals in fame, have sometimes won the prize of crowns or turned the fate of nations. But his whole career shines with the steady light of day. It has nothing to conceal, it has nothing to interpret by the flexible organs of history. Everything in it is manly, compact, and clear; shaped to one rule of public duty, animated by one passion—the love of England, and the service of the CROWN.

The Duke of WELLINGTON lived, commanded, and governed in unconscious indifference or disdainful aversion to those common incentives of human action which are derived from the powers of imagination and of sentiment. He held them cheap, both in their weakness and in their strength. The force and weight of his character stooped to no such adventitious influences. He might have kindled more enthusiasm, especially in the early and doubtful days of his Peninsular career; but in his successful and triumphant pursuit of glory her name never passed his lips, even in his addresses to his soldiers. His entire nature and character were moulded on reality. He lived to see things as they were. His acute glance and cool judgment pierced at once through the surface which entangles the imagination or kindles the sympathy of the feelings. Truth, as he loved her, is to be reached by a rougher path and by sterner minds. In war, in politics, and in the common transactions of life, the Duke of WELLINGTON adhered inflexibly to the most precise correctness in word and deed. His temperament abhorred disguises and despised exaggerations. The fearlessness of his actions was never the result of speculative confidence or foolhardy presumption, but it lay mainly in a just perception of the true relation in which he stood to his antagonists in the field or in the Senate. The greatest exploits of his life, such as the passage of the Douro, followed by the march on Madrid, the battle of Waterloo, and the passing the Catholic Relief Bill, were performed under no circumstances that could inspire enthusiasm. Nothing but the coolness of the player could have won the mighty stakes upon a cast apparently so adverse to his success. Other commanders have attained the highest pitch of glory when they disposed of the colossal resources of empires, and headed armies already flushed with the conquest of the world. The Duke of WELLINGTON found no such encouragement in any part of his career. At no time were the means at his disposal adequate to the ready and certain execution of his designs. His steady progress in the Peninsular campaigns went on against the current of fortune, till that current was itself turned by perseverance and resolution. He had a clear and complete perception of the dangers he encountered, but he saw and grasped the latent power which baffled those dangers and surmounted resistances apparently invincible. That is precisely the highest degree of courage, for it is courage conscious, enlightened, and determined.

Clearness of discernment, correctness of judgment, and rectitude in action were, without doubt, the principal elements of the Duke's brilliant achievements in war, and of his vast authority in the councils of his country, as well as in the conferences of Europe. They gave to his determinations an originality and vigour akin to that of genius, and sometimes imparted to his language in debate a pith and significance at which more brilliant orators failed to arrive. His mind, equally careless of obstacles and of effect, travelled by the shortest road to its end; and he retained, even in his latest years, all the precision with which he was wont to handle the subjects that came before him, or had at any time engrossed his attention. This was the secret of that untaught manliness and simplicity of style that pervades the vast collection of his despatches, written as they were amidst the varied cares and emotions of war; and of that lucid and appropriate mode of exposition which never failed to leave a clear impression on the minds of those whom he addressed. Other men have enjoyed, even in this age, more vivid faculties of invention and contrivance, a more extended range of foresight, a more subtle comprehension of the changing laws of society and the world. But the value of these finer perceptions, and of the policy founded upon them, has never been more assured than when it was tried and admitted by the wisdom and patriotism of that venerable mind. His superiority over other men consisted rather in the perfection of those qualities which he preeminently possessed than in the variety or extent of his other faculties.

These powers, which were unerring when applied to definite and certain facts, sometimes failed in the appreciation of causes which had not hitherto come under their observation. It is, perhaps, less to be wondered at that the soldier and the statesman of 1815, born and bred in the highest school of Tory politics, should have miscarried in his opinion of those eventful times which followed the accession of WILLIAM IV., than that the defeated opponent of Reform in 1831 should have risen into the patriot senator of 1846 and 1851. Yet the Administration of 1828, in which the Duke of WELLINGTON occupied the first and most responsible place, passed the Catholic Emancipation Act, and thereby gave the signal of a rupture in the Tory party, never afterwards entirely healed, and struck the heaviest blow on a system which the growing energies of the nation resented and condemned. Resolute to oppose what he conceived to be popular clamour, no man ever recognized with more fidelity the claims of a free nation to the gradual development of its interests and its rights; nor were his services to the cause of liberty and improvement the less great because they usually consisted in bending the will or disarming the prejudices of their fiercest opponents. Attached by birth, by character, and by opinion to the order and the cause of the British aristocracy, the Duke of WELLINGTON knew that the true power of that race of nobles lies, in this age of the world, in their inviolable attachment to constitutional principles, and their honest recognition of popular rights. Although his personal resolution and his military experience qualified him better than other men to be the champion of resistance to popular turbulence and sedition, as he showed by his preparations in May, 1832, and in April 1848, yet wisdom and forbearance were ever the handmaidens of his courage, and, while most firmly determined to defend, if necessary, the authority of the State, he was the first to set an example of conciliatory sacrifice to the reasonable claims of the nation. He was the CATULLUS of our Senate, after having been our CÆSAR in the field; and, if the commonwealth of England had ever saluted one of her citizens with the

Roman title of PARENS PATRIÆ, that touching honour would have been added to the peerage and the baton of ARTHUR WELLESLEY by the respectful gratitude and faith of the people.

Though singularly free from every trace of cant, his mind was no stranger to the sublime influence of religious truth, and he was assiduous in the observances of the public ritual of the Church of England. At times, even in the extreme period of his age, some accident would betray the deep current of feeling which he never ceased to entertain towards all that was chivalrous and benevolent. His charities were unostentatious but extensive, and he bestowed his interest throughout life upon an incredible number of persons and things which claimed his notice and solicited his aid. Every social duty, every solemnity, every ceremony, every merry-making, found him ready to take his part in it. He had a smile for the youngest child, a compliment for the prettiest face, an answer to the readiest tongue, and a lively interest in every incident of life, which it seemed beyond the power of age to chill. When time had somewhat relaxed the sterner mould of his manhood, its effects were chiefly indicated by an unabated taste for the amusements of fashionable society, incongruous at times with the dignity of extreme old age, and the recollections of so virile a career. But it seemed a part of the Duke's character that every thing that presented itself was equally welcome, for he had become a part of every thing, and it was foreign to his nature to stand aloof from any occurrence to which his presence could contribute. He seems never to have felt the flagging spirit or the reluctant step of indolence or *ennui*, or to have recoiled from any thing that remained to be done; and this complete performance of every duty, however small, as long as life remained, was the same quality which had carried him in triumph through his campaigns, and raised him to be one of the chief Ministers of England and an arbiter of the fate of Europe. It has been said that in the most active and illustrious lives there comes at last some inevitable hour of melancholy and of satiety. Upon the Duke of WELLINGTON that hour left no impression, and probably it never shed its influence over him; for he never rested on his former achievements or his length of days, but marched onwards to the end, still heading the youthful generations which had sprung into life around him, and scarcely less intent on their pursuits than they are themselves. It was a finely balanced mind to have worn so bravely and so well. When men in after times shall look back to the annals of England for examples of energy and public virtue among those who have raised this country to her station on the earth, no name will remain more conspicuous or more unsullied than that of ARTHUR WELLESLEY, THE GREAT DUKE OF WELLINGTON. The actions of his life were extraordinary, but his character was equal to his actions. He was the very type and model of an Englishman; and, though men are prone to invest the worthies of former ages with a dignity and merit they commonly withhold from their contemporaries, we can select none from the long array of our captains and our nobles who, taken for all in all, can claim a rivalry with him who is gone from amongst us, an inheritor of imperishable fame.

SIR ROBERT PEEL.

FROM THE LONDON TIMES, JULY 4, 1852.

A GREAT age has lost a great man. Sir ROBERT PEEL, whom all parties and all nations associate more than any other statesman with the policy and glory of this empire, is now a name of the past. He has been taken, as it were, from his very seat in the Senate, with nothing to prepare us for his departure, and every thing now to remind us of it, with his powers unabated, and his part unfulfilled. Although gradually removed during the last four years from the sphere of party, he had still political friends to be reconciled, a social position to be repaired, motives to be appreciated, and acts to be justified by the tardy and conflicting testimony of results. A devoted band of admirers hoped to see him set right with all the world, while life and strength still remained; and that day of peaceful triumph seemed not very distant. There were others who still saw in Sir ROBERT PEEL the man who had more than once saved his country at the cost of his party, and might again be called to a task which demanded such marvellous powers and so singular a position. The page that recorded his last great effort was scarcely spread before the eyes of the nation when the object of all these hopes and calculations was suddenly withdrawn, and they who speculate or dream over the great game of politics have to readjust their thoughts to the loss of the principal actor.

The highest possible estimate of Sir ROBERT PEEL'S services is that which we are invited to take from the mouth of his opponents. If we are to trust them, we are to believe that but for Sir ROBERT PEEL this country would long since have repudiated the exact performance of its pecuniary obligations; that half our fellow-subjects would still be excluded by their creed from office and power; and that the means of existence would still be obstructed and enhanced in their way to a teeming and industrious population. Nor can it be denied that this estimate has a very general consent in its favour. If it be asked who bound England to the faithful discharge of the largest debt ever contracted or imagined by man, and who thereby raised her credit and advanced her prosperity to an unexampled standard, one name, and one only, will present itself to the mind of either Englishman or foreigner, and that name is PEEL. If, again, it be asked who admitted eight or nine million British subjects to the rights of British citizenship, the answer still is PEEL. If, lastly, it be asked who opened the gates of trade, and bade the food of man flow hither from every shore in an uninterrupted stream, it is still PEEL who did it. On these three monuments of wisdom and beneficence other names may be written, but the name of PEEL is first and foremost. Yet they were no ordinary achievements. It is within the memory of the living generation that every one of these three things was generally thought impossible, and was wholly despaired of even by those who were most clearly convinced of their moral and political obligation. These things, too, were not done on any mean stage, but in the greatest empire of the world, and where the difficulties were in proportion to the work. But how far does the name of PEEL justly occupy this honourable position? Was he the author of these three great acts! Others, indeed, originated and proposed, for they were freer to originate, and it is always easy to gain the start of a statesman more or less implicated in existing legislation and encumbered by his supporters. But to confine ourselves to Sir ROBERT's last and crowning achievement, it must be said that while others advised the repeal of the Corn Laws when it was their interest to do so, he was the first to propose it when every thing was to be lost by it—when, in fact, he did lose every thing by it. His was the risk, so he must be the renown. His right is now proved, not by what he did, but by what he suffered, and he is the confessed author of free trade, because he has been a martyr to it. We cannot question the conscientious convictions of those who drove Sir ROBERT from power, but in so doing they testify that but for him the Corn Laws would not have been repealed.

But these acts, great as they were, and insulated as they seem, were only parts of a series, and by no means the most laborious parts. The amelioration of our criminal code, the reform of our police, the introduction of simpler forms and more responsible management into every part of our administrative system, took up large parts of Sir ROBERT's career, while there was not a subject that could possibly come within his reach that he did not grasp resolutely and well. We have had to differ from him; we do differ from him; but we must admit that no man ever undertook public affairs with a more thorough determination to leave the institutions of his country in an orderly, honest, and efficient state.

But are we wholly to pass over the ambiguities of this honourable career? Must it be left to the future historian to relate that when England lost her greatest living statesman, there were points of his character too tender to be touched, and that all parties agreed to slur over what they could not all praise? Surely not. Truth is as sacred as the grave, and the grief confessed by all may, perhaps, infuse new gravity and candour into a painful discussion. Sir Robert, so it is said, besides many smaller violences to the conscience of his followers, twice signally betrayed them. Twice he broke them up, and we now behold the result in a smitten and divided party. They gave us the most undeniable proofs that their indignation is sincere. Suicide is so frequent a form of indignant adjuration that we cannot help respecting such an evidence of wrong. But with the knell of departed greatness sounding in our ear, it is time to view these acts by the light of the future. Posterity will ask,—Were they right or were they wrong? Our own answer shall be without hesitation or reserve. They were among the most needful and salutary acts that ever were given man to do. Grant that Sir Robert compassed them unfairly, and it must at least be admitted that he had a fine taste for glory, and prized the gifts of heaven when he saw them.

But is it possible that a man should do such deeds, and a whole life full of them, and yet do them basely? To confess that were indeed a keen satire on man, if not a presumptuous imputation on his MAKER. But perhaps there is some semblance of truth in it. Take, then, the long list of earth's worthies from the beginning of story to the present hour, and let us be candid with them. It will not be easy to find many of that canonized throng, whose patriotism has not been alloyed with some baseness, who have not won triumphs with subtlety, deceived nations to their good, countermined against fraudful antagonists, or otherwise sinned against their own greatness. But when we have employed towards other men the candour imposed upon us in the case of Sir ROBERT PEEL, we find these imperfections rather a condition of humanity than a fault of the individual. Nearly all great things, even the greatest of them, have been done in this earthly fashion. In the language of purists all government is bad, Courts are corrupt, and policy a word of opprobrium. An abstract philosopher, indeed, can easily be abstractedly good, but when once we have to deal with the human material, there is no choice but to condescend.

But a charge so oft repeated, and so fixed upon the man, demands a closer scrutiny. That charge is double-dealing. It is not that Sir ROBERT was a "double-minded man," and, therefore, "unstable in his ways," but that he assembled his followers on one understanding and used them for another; or, to take a milder supposition, that he gave way to a different set of impulses, when on one side of the House, from those which swayed him on the other. Some sort of doubleness is alleged, and some sort must be conceded, though it may not be easily described. Sir ROBERT was one man by parentage, education, friends, and almost every circumstance of his very early entrance into public life, and another man by the workings of his great intellect, the expansion of his sympathies, and his vast and varied experience. He was early taught to worship GEORGE III., and to adore the very shadow of PITT, for his father published a pamphlet to prove that the National Debt was a positive source of prosperity. From this ultra-Tory household he passed to Harrow, where, as the world knows, he was the contemporary of BYRON, of ABERDEEN, and other great men; but it was at Oxford that he chiefly acquired confidence and fame. He was the most distinguished son of that University, and its most cherished representative. Thirty years ago PEEL was to do every thing for the Universities, the Church of England, the aristocracy, and every man and every thing that reposes under these institutions. The only question was, whether he would stand by them—whether he was staunch; for in those days it was the office of a statesman to do what he was bid. It is enough for our present purpose to remind our readers that he first took office under PERCEVAL, continued under Lord LIVERPOOL, ELDON all the time being Lord Chancellor; that as Irish Secretary he was early pressed into the service of the Orange party; and that meanwhile old Sir ROBERT PEEL, himself in Parliament, showed a most amiable vigilance for the integrity of his son's opinions. In fact, never was a rising young statesman blessed with so many fathers and mothers, and godfathers and godmothers. Tories and Orangemen,

Oxford and the Church, PERCEVAL and Lord LIVERPOOL, ELDON, and we believe we must add WELLINGTON, with old Sir ROBERT, to hold all together, constituted a political nursery, in which it was scarcely possible to go wrong. Unfortunately for his numerous patrons and advisers, PEEL had something else in him than a capacity for receiving nursery impressions. He was a great man, and broke through his trammels, but his life was spent in that long and painful struggle. His affections, his friendships, his pledges and his speeches, kept in record against him, held him back, while his far-seeing and active solicitude for his country drew him on. His life was one long contest, for warm pledges are not easily broken, nor, on the other hand, are deep convictions easily belied. But is it impossible for a really honest man to suffer such a struggle? All history and every man's own experience will tell him that it is not impossible. The larger a man's capacity, and the kindlier his nature, the wider also will be his sympathies; and the more likely also will he be to embrace and feel many conflicting considerations. His heart may draw him one way and his reason another. The influence of a sudden event, the force of some new argument, the excitement of some discussion, the persuasion of some example may ever and anon take possession of the imagination and senses, while the mind within pursues its even tenor, finds out truth at last, and then holds it fast. But the age wherein we live is interested in vindicating the character of its own statesmen. Be he double or single, Sir ROBERT PEEL was the type and representative of his generation. We have lived in a period of transition, and Sir ROBERT has conducted us safely through it. England has changed as well as he.

Sir ROBERT has died "in harness." He never sought repose, and his almost morbid restlessness rendered him incapable of enjoying it. His was a life of effort. The maxim that if any thing is worth doing, it is worth doing well, seemed ever present to his mind, so that every thing he did or said was somewhat over-laboured. His official powers, as some one said the other day, were Atlantean, and his Ministerial expositions on the same gigantic scale. There was an equal appearance of effort, however, in his most casual remarks, at least when in public, for he would never throw away a chance; and he still trusted to his industry rather than to his powers. But a man whose life is passed in the service of the public, and whose habits are Parliamentary or official, is not to be judged by ordinary rules, for he can scarcely fail to be cold, guarded, and ostentatious. What is a senate but a species of theatre, where a part must be acted, feelings must be expressed, and applause must be won? Undoubtedly the habit of political exhibition told on Sir ROBERT's manner and style, and even on his mind. His egotism was proverbial, but besides the excessive use of the first person, it occasionally betrayed him into performances at variance both with prudence and taste. His love of applause was closely allied to a still more dangerous appetite for national prosperity, without sufficient regard to its sources and permanence. It was this that seduced him into encouraging, instead of controlling the railway mania. Had the opportunity been allowed, we are inclined to think he would have falsified the common opinion as to his excessive discretion, and astonished mankind with some splendid, if successful, novelties. His style of speaking was admirably adapted for its purpose, for it was luminous and methodical, while his powerful voice and emphatic delivery gave almost too much assistance to his language, for it was apt to be redundant and commonplace. He had not that strong simplicity of expression which is almost a tradition of the old Whig school, and is no slight element of its power. We had almost omitted Sir ROBERT's private character. This is not the place to trumpet private virtues, which never shine better than when they are really private. Suffice it to say that Sir ROBERT was honoured and beloved in every relation of private life.

Such is the man, the statesman, and the patriot, with his great virtues, and perhaps his little failings, that has fallen at his post. Under PROVIDENCE he has been our chief guide from the confusions and darkness that hung round the beginning of this century to the comparatively quiet haven in which we are now embayed. Under the lamentable circumstances of his departure, we again revert with renewed satisfaction to the speech which, little as he thought it, was his farewell to the nation. Not the least prominent or least pleasing portion of that speech was its calm, retrospective, and conciliatory character, and, in particular, the manner in which he unconsciously took leave of the man, whose policy he stood up to review, and who had entered public life with him, under the same master, forty-one years ago. Having in his introductory sentences declared his cordial concurrence with many parts of the Ministerial policy during their whole period of office, when he came at last to speak of the course recently taken by our diplomacy, he observed,—"I have so little disposition—and I say it with truth, for the feelings which have actuated me for the last four years remain unabated (hear, hear)—I have so little disposition, I say, for entering into any angry or hostile controversy, that I shall make no reference whatever to many of the topics which were introduced into that most able and most temperate speech, which made us proud of the man who delivered it (loud and general cheering), and in which he vindicated with becoming spirit, and with an ability worthy of his name and place, that course of conduct which he had pursued. (Cheers.") The man who said this had his heart in the right place, and no reconciliation forced by the agonies, the terrors, or the weakness of a deathbed ever exceeded the feeling of that simple and spontaneous acknowledgment. Sir Robert, it is a comfort to think, has left us with words of peace and candour on his lips, and that same peace and candour, we cannot help believing, will be awarded to his memory by his own political opponents.

BIOGRAPHY OF

SIR ROBERT PEEL.

In the following brief narrative of the principal facts in the life of the great statesman who has just been snatched from among us, we must disclaim all intention of dealing with his biography in any searching or ambitious spirit. The national loss is so great, the bereavement so sudden, that we cannot sit down calmly either to eulogize or arraign the memory of the deceased. We cannot forget that it was not a week ago wo were occupied in recording and commenting upon his last eloquent address to that Assembly which had so often listened with breathless attention to his statesmanlike expositions of policy. We freely confess, too, that, however much under ordinary circumstances we feel it our duty to be prepared with such information as is most likely to interest the public, the death of poor Sir Robert Peel was an exceptional case. It was too revolting to prepare the biography of so great a man while he was yet alive—crushed and mangled indeed, and with little hope of recovery—but still alive. We could do little else when the mournful intelligence reached us that Sir Robert Peel was no more, than pen a few expressions of sorrow and respect. Even now the following imperfect record of facts, prepared, as it has been, in the course of a few hours, must be accepted as a poor substitute for the biography of that great Englishman, whose loss will be felt almost as a private bereavement by every family throughout the British Empire.

Sir Robert Peel was in the 63d year of his age, having been born near Bury, in Lancashire, on the 5th of February, 1788. His father was a manufacturer on a grand scale, and a man of much natural ability, and of almost unequalled opulence. Full of a desire to render his son and probable successor worthy of the influence and the vast wealth which he had to bestow, the first Sir Robert Peel took the utmost pains personally with the early training of the future Prime Minister. He retained his son under his own immediate superintendence, until he arrived at a sufficient age to be sent to Harrow. Mr. Robert Peel went to Harrow certainly a ready recipient of scholarship, but by no means an advanced schoolboy. From the outset he was assiduous, docile, and submissive, yet in the prompt and vigorous performance of school duties he lagged for a time behind boys who in every thing but experience were infinitely his inferiors. This, however, was only a temporary check at the threshold of a great career. He advanced rapidly and securely, and soon left all competition in the rear; but he wanted the animal energy and buoyancy of spirit which give pre-eminence out of school. Lord Byron, his contemporary at Harrow, was a better declaimer and a more amusing actor, but in sound learning and laborious application to school duties young Peel had no equal. So marked was his superiority in these respects that the unanimous opinion of the little senate to which he then gave laws was, that he could not fail to be a Cabinet Minister at an early age. Masters and scholars shared this sentiment. He had scarcely completed his sixteenth year when he left Harrow and became a gentleman commoner of Christ Church, Oxford, where he took the degree of A. B., in Michaelmas Term, 1808, with unprecedented distinction. Advisedly it may be said that his success was unprecedented, for the present system of examination being then new, no man before his time ever took the honours of a double first class—first in classics, first in mathematics. It did so happen that Mr. Peel was the first recipient of that much-prized object of youthful ambition.

The year 1809 saw him attain his majority, and saw him also take his seat in the House of Commons as member for the ancient city of Cashel, in the county of Tipperary—a place not then returning the nominee of the popular party in Ireland, but the man who, on account of party interests or other considerations, could find favour in the sight of Mr. Richard Pennefather, who, in the phraseology of that day, "had the patronage of Cashel." Whether similarity of opinion in matters political, or a more direct influence, may have led to Mr. Peel's being member for Cashel, one need not at this distance of time too minutely inquire. Whatever may have been the consideration, the twelve voters of Cashel (then the only electors in that city) enjoyed his first services in Parliament, and continued to call him their member till the general election in

1812, when he came in for Chippenham, a Wiltshire borough, where he acquired—probably by means similar to those used at Cashel—the honour of a seat in Parliament. The main difference between the two boroughs consisted in the fact that in the former case he had only 12 constituents, in the latter 135.

The first Sir Robert Peel had long been a member of the House of Commons, and the early efforts of his son in that assembly were regarded with considerable interest not only on account of his University reputation, but also because he was the son of such a father. He did not, however, begin public life by staking his fame on the results of one elaborate oration; on the contrary, he rose now and then on comparatively unimportant occasions; made a few brief modest remarks, stated a fact or two, explained a difficulty when he happened to understand the matter in hand better than others, and then sat down without taxing too severely the patience or good-nature of an auditory accustomed to great performances. Still in the second year of his Parliamentary course he ventured to make a set speech, when, at the commencement of the session of 1810, he seconded the address in reply to the King's speech. Thenceforward for 19 years a more highflying Tory than Mr. Peel was not to be found within the walls of Parliament. Lord Eldon applauded him as a young and valiant champion of those abuses in the State which were then fondly called "the institutions of the country;" Lord Sidmouth regarded him as his rightful political heir, and even the Duke of Cumberland patronized Mr. Peel. He further became the favourite *elève* of Mr. Perceval, then first Lord of the

Treasury, and entered office as Under-Secretary for the Home Department. Mr. Richard Ryder, uncle of the present Earl of Harrowby, was at that time the principal Secretary. He continued in the Home Department for two years, not often speaking in Parliament, but rather qualifying himself for those prodigious labours in debate, in council, and in office, which it has since been his lot to encounter and perform.

In the month of May, 1812, Mr. Perceval fell by the hand of an assassin, and the composition of the Ministry necessarily underwent a great change. The result, so far as Mr. Peel was concerned, was that he was appointed Chief Secretary to the Lord-Lieutenant of Ireland. This was an office which in those days, and long afterwards, it was the practice of successive Governments to confer upon the most promising of the youthful members of their party. Mr. Peel had only reached his 24th year when, in the month of September, 1812, the duties of that anxious and laborious position were intrusted to his hands. The late Duke of Richmond held the office of Viceroy, and Mr. Vesey Fitzgerald, afterwards Lord Fitzgerald, that of Chancellor of the Exchequer for Ireland. The Legislative Union was then but lately consummated, and the demand for Catholic emancipation had given rise to an agitation of only very recent date. But in proportion to its novelty so was its vigour. Mr. Peel was, therefore, as the representative of the old Tory Protestant school, called upon to encounter a storm of unpopularity such as not even an Irish Secretary has ever been exposed to. No term of reproach was too strong; no amount of obloquy considered disproportioned to the high enormities which the Roman Catholic party charged upon him whom they would never call by any other appellation than "Orange Peel." That he bore it all with becoming fortitude, and resented it as often as it was safe to do so, is no more than the subsequent course of his life would lead one to expect. But he sometimes went a little further, and condescended personally to take notice of the offensive violence which marked the course of Irish opposition. The late Mr. O'Connell at various public meetings, and in various forms, through the agency of the press, poured forth upon Mr. Peel a torrent of invective, which went beyond even his extraordinary performances in the science of scolding. At length he received from Mr. Peel a communication in the shape of a hostile message. Sir Charles Saxton, who was Under-Secretary in Ireland, had an interview first with Mr. O'Connell and afterwards with a friend of that gentleman, a Mr Lidwell. Negotiations went on for three or four days, when Mr. O'Connell was taken into custody and bound over to keep the peace towards all his fellow-subjects in Ireland. Mr. Peel and his friend immediately came to this country, and subsequently proceeded to the continent. Mr. O'Connell followed them to London, but the police were active enough to bring him before the Chief Justice of England, when he entered into recognizances to keep the peace towards all His Majesty's subjects; and so ended one of the few personal squabbles in which Mr. Peel had ever been engaged. For six years he held the office of Chief Secretary to the Lord-Lieutenant, at a time when the government was conducted upon what might be called "anti-conciliation principles." The opposite course was commenced by Mr. Peel's immediate successor, Mr. Charles Grant, now Lord Glenelg. That a Chief Secretary so circumstanced, struggling to sustain extreme Orangeism in its dying agonies, should have been called upon to encounter great toil and anxiety, is a truth too obvious to need illustration. That in these straits Mr. Peel acquitted himself with infinite address was as readily acknowledged at that time as it has ever been even in the zenith of his fame. He introduced and defended many Irish measures, including some peace-preservation bills. The establishment of the constabulary force in that country has, however, been amongst the most permanent results of his administration. It is, moreover, one which may be considered as the experimental or preliminary step to the introduction of that system of metropolitan police, which gives security to person and property amidst the congregated millions of the vast cluster of cities, boroughs, and villages which we call "London," and which has since been extended to every considerable provincial town. The minor measures of Sir Robert Peel's administration in Ireland possess, at this distance of time, but few features of interest to readers who live in the year 1850. He held office in that country under three successive Viceroys, the Duke of Richmond, Earl Whitworth, and Earl Talbot, all of whom have long since passed away from this life, their names and their deeds alike forgotten. But the history of their Chief Secretary happens not to have been composed of such perishable materials, and we now approach one of the most memorable passages of his eventful career. He was Chairman of the great Bullion Committee ; but before he engaged in that s· dous task he had resigned the Chief-Secretarysh. Ireland. As a consequence of the report of that committee, he took charge of and introduced the bill for authorizing a return to cash payments which bears his name, and which measure received the sanction of Parliament in the year 1819. That measure brought upor Mr. Peel no slight or temporary odium. The first Sir Robert Peel was then alive, and altogether differed from his son as to the tendency of his measure. It was roundly asserted at the time, and very faintly denied, that it rendered that gentleman a more wealthy man, by something like half a million sterling, than he had previously been. The deceased statesman, however, must in common justice be acquitted of any sinister purpose.

This narrative now reaches the year 1820, when we have to relate the only domestic event in the history of Sir Robert Peel which requires notice. On the 8th of June, at Upper Seymour-street, London, being then in the 33d year of his age, he married Julia, daughter of General Sir John Floyd, who had then attained the age of 25.

Two years afterwards there was a lull in public affairs, which gave somewhat the appearance of tranquillity ; Lord Sidmouth was growing old, he thought that his system was successful, and that at length he might find repose. He considered it then consistent with his public duty to consign to younger and stronger hands the seals of the Home Department. He accepted a seat in the Cabinet without office, and continued to give his support to Lord Liverpool, his ancient political

In permitting his mantle to fall upon Mr. Peel, he thought he was assisting to invest with authority one whose views and policy were as narrow as his own, and whose practice in carrying them out would be not less rigid and uncompromising. But, like many others, he lived long enough to be grievously disappointed by the subsequent career of him whom the Liberal party have since called "the great Minister of progress," and whom their opponents have not scrupled to designate by appellations too harsh to be repeated in these hours of sorrow and bereavement. On the 17th January, 1822, Mr. Peel was installed at the head of the Home Department, where he remained undisturbed till the political demise of Lord Liverpool in the spring of 1827. And here for a moment the narrative of his official life may be interrupted, in order to remind the reader that he did not always represent in Parliament such insignificant places as Cashel and Chippenham. The most distinguished man that has filled the Chair of the House of Commons in the present century was Charles Abbott, afterwards Lord Colchester. In the summer of 1817 this gentleman had completed 16 years of hard service in that most eminent office, and he had represented the University of Oxford for 11 years. His valuable labours having been rewarded with a pension and a peerage, he took his seat, full of years and honours, among the hereditary legislators of the land, and left a vacancy in the representation of his *alma mater*, which Mr. Peel above all living men was deemed the most fitting person to occupy. At that time he was an intense Tory—or as the Irish called him, an Orange Protestant of the deepest dye—one prepared to make any sacrifice for the maintenance of Church and State as established by the Revolution of 1688. Who, therefore, so fit as he to represent the loyalty, learning, and orthodoxy of Oxford? To have done so had been the object of Mr. Canning's young ambition, but in 1817 he could not be so ungrateful to Liverpool as to reject its representation even for the early object of his Parliamentary affections. Mr. Peel, therefore, was returned in the month of June, without opposition, for that constituency which many consider the most important in the land—a constituency with which Mr. Peel remained on the best possible terms for an unbroken period of 12 years. The question of the repeal of the penal laws affecting the Roman Catholics, which severed so many political connexions, was, however, destined to separate Mr. Peel from Oxford. In the year 1828 rumours of the coming change were rife, and many expedients were devised to extract from Mr. Secretary Peel his opinions on the Catholic question. But with the impenetrable reserve which ever marked his character he baffled inquiry and left all curiosity at fault. At last the hard necessities of the Government rendered further concealment impossible, and out came the frightful truth that Mr. Peel was no longer an Orangeman. The ardent friends who had frequently supported his Oxford elections, and the hot partisans who shouted "Peel and Protestantism" at the Brunswick Clubs, reviled him for his defection in no measured terms. On the 4th of February, 1829, he addressed a letter to the Vice-Chancellor of Oxford, stating in many well-turned phrases that the Catholic question must be forthwith adjusted, under advice in which he concurred; and that, therefore, he considered himself bound to resign that trust which the University had during so many years confided to his hands. Mr. Peel's resignation was accepted; but as the avowed purpose of that important step was to give to his constituents an opportunity of pronouncing an opinion upon a change of policy, he merely accepted the Chiltern Hundreds with the intention of immediately becoming a candidate for that seat in Parliament which he had just vacated. At this election Mr. Peel was opposed by Sir Robert Inglis, who was elected by 755 to 609. Mr. Peel was therefore obliged to cast himself on the favour of Sir Mannasseh Lopez, who returned him for the borough of Westbury in Wiltshire, which undignified constituency he continued to represent during two years, until at the general election in 1830, he was chosen for Tamworth, in the representation for which borough he has continued for exactly 20 years.

The main feature of his official life still remains to be noticed. With the exception of Lord Palmerston, no statesman of modern times has spent so many years in the civil service of the Crown as Sir Robert Peel. If no account be taken of the short time he was engaged upon the Bullion Committee, in effecting the change in the currency, and in opposing for a few months the Ministries of Mr. Canning and Lord Goderich, it may be stated that from 1810 to 1830 he formed part of the Government, and presided over it as First Minister in 1834–5, as well as from 1841 to 1846 inclusive. During the time that he held the office of Home Secretary, under Lord Liverpool, he effected many important changes in the administration of domestic affairs, and many legislative improvements of a practical and comprehensive character. But his fame as a member of Parliament was principally sustained at this period of his life by the extensive and admirable alterations which he effected in the criminal law. Romily and Mackintosh had preceded him in the great work of reforming and humanizing the code of England. For his hand, however, was reserved the introduction of ameliorations which they had long toiled and struggled for in vain. The Ministry, through whose influence he was enabled to carry these salutary reforms, lost its chief in the person of Lord Liverpool, during the early part of the year 1827. When Mr. Canning undertook to form a government, Mr. Peel, the late Lord Eldon, the Duke of Wellington, and other eminent Tories of that day, threw up office, and are said to have persecuted Mr. Canning with a degree of rancour far outstripping the legitimate bounds of political hostility. At least those were the sentiments expressed by some of the less discreet friends of Mr. Canning. It was certainly the opinion held by the late Lord George Bentinck, when he said that "they hounded to death my illustrious relative;" and the ardour of his subsequent opposition to Sir Robert Peel evidently derived its intensity from a long cherished sense of the injuries supposed to have been inflicted upon Mr. Canning. In the language of Lord George Bentinck, and in that of many others who had not the excuse of private friendship, there was much of exaggeration, if not of absolute error. It is the opinion of men not ill informed respecting the sentiments of Canning, that he considered Peel as his true political successor—as a statesman competent to the task of working out that large and liberal policy which he fondly hoped the Tories might, however tardily, be induced to sanction. At all events, he is believed not to have entertained towards Mr. Peel any personal hostility, and to have stated during his short-lived tenure of office that that gentleman was the only member of his party who had not treated him with ingratitude and unkindness.

In the month of January, 1828, the Wellington Ministry took office and held it till November, 1830. Mr. Peel's reputation suffered during this period very rude shocks. He gave up, as already stated, his anti-Catholic principles, lost the force of twenty years' consistency, and under unheard of disadvantages introduced the very measure he had spent so many years in opposing. The debates upon Catholic Emancipation, which preceded the great Reform question, constituted a period in the life of Sir Robert Peel, which, twenty years ago, every one would have considered its chief and prominent feature. There can be no doubt that the course he then adopted, demanded greater moral courage than at any previous period of his life he had been called upon to exercise. He believed himself incontestably in the right; he believed, with the Duke of Wellington, that the danger of civil war was imminent, and that such an event was immeasurably a greater evil than surrendering the boasted constitution of 1688. But he was called upon to snap asunder a Parliamentary connexion of twelve years with a great University, in which the most interesting period of his youth had been passed; he was called upon to encounter the reproaches of adherents, whom he had often led in well-fought contests against the advocates of what was termed "civil and religious liberty;" he had further to tell the world, that the character of public men for consistency, however precious, is not to be directly opposed to the common weal; and to communicate to many the novel, as well as unpalatable, truth, that what they deemed "principle" must give way to what he called "expediency." It is to be expected, however, that posterity will do him the justice to acknowledge that, if he accomplished much, he suffered much in the performance of what he believed to be his highest duties.

When he ceased to be a Minister of the Crown, that general movement throughout Europe which succeeded the deposition of the elder branch of the Bourbons rendered Parliamentary reform as unavoidable as two years previously Catholic emancipation had been. He opposed this change, no doubt with increased knowledge and matured talents, but with impaired influence and few Parliamentary followers. The history of the reform debates will show that Mr. (then Sir Robert) Peel made many admirable speeches which served to raise his reputation, but never for a moment turned the tide of fortune against his adversaries, and in the first session of the first reformed Parliament he found himself at the head of a party that in numbers little exceeded one hundred. As soon as it was practicable he rallied his broken forces; either he or some of his political friends gave them the name of "Conservatives," and it required but a short interval of reflection and observation to prove to his sagacious intellect that the period of reaction was at hand. Every engine of party organization was put into vigorous activity, and before the summer of 1834 reached its close he was at the had of a compact, powerful, and well-disciplined Opposition. Such a high impression of their vigour and efficiency had King William IV. received, that when, in November, Lord Althorp became a peer, and the Whigs therefore lost their leader in the House of Commons, His Majesty sent to Italy to summon Sir Robert Peel to his councils with a view to the immediate formation of a Conservative Ministry. Sir Robert accepted this heavy responsibility, though he thought that the King had grievously mistaken the condition of the country and the chances of success which awaited his political friends. A new House of Commons was instantly called, and for nearly three months Sir Robert Peel maintained a gallant struggle against the most formidable opposition that for nearly a century past any Minister has been called upon to encounter. At no time did his command of temper, his almost exhaustless resources of information, his vigorous and comprehensive intellect appear to create such astonishment or draw forth expressions of such unbounded admiration as in the early part of the year 1835. But, after a well-fought contest, he retired once more into opposition till the close of the second Melbourne Administration in 1841. It was in the month of April, 1835, that Lord Melbourne was restored to power, but the continued enjoyment of office did not much promote the political interests of his party, and from various causes the power of the Whigs began to decline. The commencement of a new reign gave them some popularity, but in the new House of Commons, elected in consequence of that event, the Conservative party were evidently gaining strength; still, after the failure of 1834–5, it was no easy task to dislodge an existing Ministry, and at the same time to be prepared with a Cabinet and a party competent to succeed them. Sir Robert Peel, therefore, with characteristic caution, "bided his time," conducting the business of Opposition throughout the whole of this period with an ability and success of which history affords few examples. He had accepted the Reform Bill as the established law of England, and as the system upon which the country was thenceforward to be governed. He was willing to carry it out in its true spirit, but he would proceed no further. He marshalled his Opposition upon the principle of resistance to any further organic changes, and he enlisted the majority of the peers and nearly the whole of the country gentlemen of England in support of the great principle of protection to British industry. The little manœuvres and small political intrigues of the period are almost forgotten, and the remembrance of them is scarcely worthy of revival. It may, however, be mentioned that in 1839 Ministers, being left in a minority, resigned, and Sir Robert Peel, when sent for by the Queen, demanded that certain ladies in the household of Her Majesty, —the near relatives of eminent Whig politicians,—should be removed from the personal service of the Sovereign. As this was refused, he abandoned for the time any attempt to form a Government, and his opponents remained in office till September, 1841. It was then Sir Robert Peel became First Lord of the Treasury, and the Duke of Wellington, without office, accepted a seat in the Cabinet, taking the management of the House of Lords. His Ministry was formed emphatically on Protectionist principles, but the close of its career was marked by the adoption of free trade doctrines in the widest and most liberal sense. We do not here propose to re-open a question already decided, but to record the fact that Sir Robert Peel's sense of public duty impelled him once more to incur the odium and obloquy which attend a fundamental change of policy, and a repudiation of the political partisans by whose ardent support a Minister may have attained office and authority. It was his sad fate to encounter more than any man ever did of that most painful hostility which such conduct, however necessary, never fails to produce. This great change in our commercial policy, however unavoidable, must be regarded as the proximate cause of Sir Robert Peel's final expulsion from office in the month of July, 1846. His administration, however, had been signalized by several measures of great political importance. Among the earliest and most prominent of these were his financial plans, the striking feature of which was an income-tax; greatly extolled for the exemption it afforded from other burdens pressing more severely on industry, but loudly condemned for its irregular and unequal operation, a vice which has since rendered its contemplated increase impossible.

Of the Ministerial life of Sir Robert Peel little more remains to be related, except that which properly belongs rather to the history of the country than to his individual biography. But it would be unjust to the memory of one of the most sagacious statesmen that England ever produced, to deny that his latest renunciation of political principles required but two short years to attest the vital necessity of that unqualified surrender. If the corn laws had been in existence at the period when the political system of the Continent was shaken to its centre and dynasties crumbled into dust, a question would have been left in the hands of the democratic party of England, the force of which neither skill nor influence could then have evaded. Instead of broken friendships, shattered reputations for consistency, or diminished rents, the whole realm of England might have borne a fearful share in that storm of wreck and revolution which had its crisis on the 10th of April, 1848.

In the course of his long and eventful life many honours were conferred upon Sir Robert Peel. Wherever he went, and almost at all times, he attracted universal attention, and was always received with the highest consideration. At the close of the year 1836, the University of Glasgow elected him their Lord Rector; and the Conservatives of that city in January, 1837, invited him to a banquet at which 3,000 gentlemen assembled to do honour to their great political chief. But this was only one among many occasions on which he was "the great guest." Perhaps the most remarkable of these banquets was that given to him in 1835, at Merchant Tailors' Hall, by 300 members of the House of Commons. Many other circumstances might be related to illustrate the high position which Sir Robert Peel occupied in this country. Anecdotes innumerable might be recorded to show the extraordinary influence in Parliament which made him "the great commoner" of the age; for Sir Robert Peel was not only a skilful and adroit debater, but by many degrees the most able and one of the most eloquent men in either house of Parliament. Nothing could be more stately or imposing than the long array of sounding periods in which he expounded his doctrines, assailed his political adversaries, or vindicated his own policy. But when the whole land laments his loss, when England mourns the untimely fate of one of her noblest sons, the task of critical disquisition upon literary attainments or public oratory possesses little attraction. It may be left for calmer moments, and a more distant time, to investigate with unforgiving justice the sources of his errors, or to estimate the precise value of services which the public is now disposed to regard with no other feelings than those of unmingled gratitude.

THE END.

THACKERAY (the author of "Vanity Fair"), the late ROBERT SOUTHEY, JOHN FORSTER, SIR HUMPHREY DAVY, JOHN WILSON ("Christopher North" of Blackwood), WALTER SAVAGE LANDOR, the Writers for the LONDON TIMES, the leading QUARTERLY REVIEWS, LEIGH HUNT, the late WILLIAM HAZLITT, the authors of the "Rejected Addresses," BARHAM (author of the "Ingoldsby Legends"), SIR FRANCIS HEAD, JAMES MONTGOMERY, &c., &c., comprising generally the most brilliant authors of the Nineteenth Century.

APPLETONS' POPULAR LIBRARY will be printed uniformly in a very elegant and convenient 16mo. form, in volumes of from 250 to 400 pages each, from new type and on superior paper, and will be *bound* in a novel and attractive style for preservation, in fancy cloth, and will be sold at the average price of fifty cents per volume.

The following books, indicating the variety of the series, are preparing for immediate publication; and orders of the Trade are solicited:—

ESSAYS: A SERIES OF PERSONAL AND HISTORICAL SKETCHES FROM THE LONDON TIMES.

LIFE AND MISCELLANIES OF THEODORE HOOK.

JOHN FORSTER'S LIFE OF GOLDSMITH.

THE YELLOWPLUSH PAPERS AND OTHER VOLUMES, BY WILLIAM M. THACKERAY, AUTHOR OF "VANITY FAIR."

JEREMY TAYLOR; A BIOGRAPHY, BY ROBERT ARIS WILLMOTT.

LEIGH HUNT'S BOOK FOR A CORNER.

THE MISCELLANEOUS WRITINGS OF JAMES AND HORACE SMITH, THE AUTHORS OF THE "REJECTED ADDRESSES."

THE INGOLDSBY LEGENDS, BY BARHAM.

LITTLE PEDLINGTON AND THE PEDLINGTONIANS BY JOHN POOLE, AUTHOR OF "PAUL PRY."

&c., &c., &c

APPLETONS' POPULAR LIBRARY.

THE MAIDEN AND MARRIED LIFE OF MARY POWELL,

AFTERWARDS MISTRESS MILTON.

Price Fifty Cents

"A reproduction "in their manners as they lived" of John Milton and his young bride, of whom the anecdote of their separation and reconciliation is told in Dr. Johnson's biography of the poet. The narrative is in the style of the period as the Diary of Lady Willoughby is written, and is remarkable for its feminine grace and character—and the interest of real life artistically disposed: a book for the selected shelf of the lady's boudoir in its touches of nature and sentiment no less than as a study of one of England's greatest poets "at home."

ENGLISH NOTICES.

"This is a charming book; and whether we regard its subject, cleverness or delicacy of sentiment and expression, it is likely to be a most acceptable present to young or old, be their peculiar taste for religion, morals, poetry, history, or romance."—*Christian Observer.*

"Unquestionably the production of an able hand, and a refined mind. We recommend it to all who love pure, healthy literary fare."—*Church and State Gazette.*

"Full of incident and character, and exceedingly delightful in its happy sketching and freshness of feeling. It is by far the best work of the small and novel class to which it belongs, a mixture of truth and fiction in a form which belongs to the fictitious more than to the substantial contents."—*Nonconformist.*

"The odd history of Milton's first marriage—the desertion of his wife, and her subsequent terror when she heard that he was just the man to put in practice his own opinions respecting divorce—forms one of those chapters, peculiarly open to illustration and fancy."—*Atlas.*

www.ingramcontent.com/pod-product-compliance
Lightning Source LLC
LaVergne TN
LVHW011207110826
845150LV00006B/1348